A FAMILY HAGGADAH

II

A Seder Service For All Ages

Shoshana Silberman

Illustrated by
Katherine Janus Kahn

KAR-BEN
PUBLISHING

With thanks to my superb editors, Judye Groner and Madeline Wikler, who gave me a second opportunity to study and write about the Passover seder.

With gratitude to our children, their spouses, and our grandchildren for helping us to continue the tradition of lively sedarim.

With love to my husband Mel for advice, support, and inspiration.

With tears for Bubbe – Grandma Betty Ribner Borak z"l – whom we miss at our family seder.

To all of you, *A Family Haggadah II* is dedicated.

KAR-BEN PUBLISHING
A division of Lerner Publishing Group, Inc.
241 First Avenue North
Minneapolis, MN 55401 USA
1-800-4KARBEN

Website Address: www.karben.com

Library of Congress Cataloging-in-Publication Data

Shoshana Silberman
A Family Haggadah II / Shoshana Silberman : illustrated by Katherine Janus Kahn.
p. cm.
"The seder service with English and Hebrew texts and prayers, and gender-sensitive translations, is provided on the right-hand pages. Commentaries and discussion questions are on the left'hand pages." —Introd.
ISBN-13: 978–0–929371–96–2 (softcover)
ISBN-10: 0–929371–96–8 (softcover)
ISBN-13: 978–1–58013–014–1 (softcover, large print edition)
ISBN-10: 1–58013–014–3 (softcover, large print edition)
ISBN-13: 978–0–7613–5211–2 (softcover, rev.)
ISBN-13: 978–0–7613–6028–5 (softcover, large print edition, rev.)
1. Haggadot—Texts. 2. Seder—Liturgy—Texts. 3. Judaism—Liturgy—Texts. I. Silberman, Shoshana. II. title.
BM674.75.S55 1997
296.4'5371—dc21 96-50284

978-0-7613-6028-5 (pbk.)

Manufactured in the United States of America
5-1013349-11413-9/30/2025

INTRODUCTION

A Family Haggadah II joins *A Family Haggadah* as a vehicle to enliven your seder and enhance its meaning. It includes all new commentaries and discussion questions from traditional and contemporary sources, and speaks to people of various backgrounds and levels of knowledge. You may wish to use it as your new haggadah of choice, or as a change of pace for your second (third or fourth!) nights' celebration.

Haggadah means "telling." It became known as the seder text because of the Biblical verse: "*Ve'higadeta l'vincha* . . . And you shall tell it to your child." The text is over 2000 years old. During this time, prayers, hymns, and selections from the Mishnah were added. By the Middle Ages, it was recorded as an addition to the prayerbook. In the 13th century, it became a separate, handwritten book. For the last five centuries, Haggadot have been printed . . . often with beautiful illustrations.

Today, there are over 3,500 Haggadot in many languages, and the number is growing. Although the core is the same, the story is often retold from different points of view, in keeping with the notion that "in every generation, everyone must think of himself or herself as having personally left Egypt."

The format of *A Family Haggadah II: A Seder Service For All Ages* is similar to *A Family Haggadah I: For Families With Young Children*. The seder service, with English and Hebrew texts and gender-sensitive translations, is provided on the right-hand pages. Commentaries and discussion questions are on the left-hand pages. There are choices to enable participants to find topics of interest to them. In response to suggestions, we have included the complete *Birkat Hamazon* (Blessing after the Meal). *A Family Haggadah II* does not have activities for very young childen, but is geared to ages pre-teen through adult. We suggest you look through the text beforehand and select the topics you wish to discuss. Do not attempt to discuss every question; leave some for seders to come!

In Exodus 10:9 it says "We will go with our young and our old . . . our sons and our daughters . . . to observe a festival to Adonai." Passover is an inclusive holiday. Family and friends of all ages should be welcomed and encouraged to join in the songs and prayers.

THE SEDER PLATE

Ashkenazim (Jews of European ancestry) make charoset from chopped apples, nuts, and cinnamon (and sometimes a touch of honey). Sephardim (Jews descended from Spain and Portugal) use dates, figs, and nuts. Some Israelis add bananas. All use red wine to give it a brick-like color.

To make the seder plate more beautiful, purchase a fresh horseradish three weeks prior to Passover. Cut off the heavy, knot-like head, keeping about an inch. Place the head in a shallow dish with a little water that is replenished daily. Lovely green shoots will sprout![1]

It has become a tradition to put out a cup of fresh water for Miriam along with the cup for Elijah, to honor her for being a fountain of strength for the Jewish people. We have included an "invitation" for Miriam to join us (page 49).

SEDER CHECKLIST

Holiday candles
Wine or grape juice
Seder Plate
Cup of Wine for Elijah
Miriam's Cup
Three matzot, covered
Pillow(s) for reclining
Salt water for dipping
Cup, basin, towel
Haggadah for each person
Wine cup for each person

Optional:

Matzah of Hope
Afikomen Bag
Flowers
Individual seder plates with karpas, maror, charoset
Empty plate to remember the homeless
An orange as a symbol of inclusivity[2]
A dish of olives as a symbol of peace

SEDER PLATE

BEITZAH	Roasted egg*	בֵּיצָה
KARPAS	Parsley, celery, potato	כַּרְפַּס
Z'ROA	Roasted bone*	זְרוֹעַ
CHAROSET	Chopped apples and nuts	חֲרֹסֶת
MAROR	Bitter herb (whole or grated horseradish or romaine lettuce)	מָרוֹר
CHAZERET	Second bitter herb for Hillel sandwich	חֲזֶרֶת

*Vegetarians may wish to substitute an avocado seed and beet instead.

WE LIGHT THE CANDLES

Before sunset, light candles and say this blessing:
(On Shabbat, add the words in brackets)

בָּרוּךְ אַתָּה יְיָ אֱלֹהֵינוּ מֶלֶךְ הָעוֹלָם אֲשֶׁר קִדְּשָׁנוּ בְּמִצְוֹתָיו וְצִוָּנוּ לְהַדְלִיק נֵר שֶׁל (שַׁבָּת וְשֶׁל) יוֹם טוֹב.

Baruch Atah Adonai Eloheinu melech ha'olam, asher kid'shanu b'mitzvotav v'tzivanu l'hadlik ner shel [Shabbat v'shel] Yom Tov.

We praise You, Adonai our God, Ruler of the Universe, Who makes us holy by Your mitzvot and commands us to light the [Sabbath and] festival lights.

בָּרוּךְ אַתָּה יְיָ אֱלֹהֵינוּ מֶלֶךְ הָעוֹלָם שֶׁהֶחֱיָנוּ וְקִיְּמָנוּ וְהִגִּיעָנוּ לַזְּמַן הַזֶּה.

Baruch Atah Adonai Eloheinu melech ha'olam, shehecheyanu v'kiy'manu v'higianu lazman hazeh.

We praise You, Adonai our God, Ruler of the Universe, Who has kept us alive and well so that we can celebrate this special time.

It is customary to say a personal prayer after lighting the Shabbat and Festival candles. On this seder night, what prayer is in your heart?

THE SEDER HAS A SPECIAL ORDER

SEDER means order. Here is the SEDER of the SEDER:

KADDESH	We say the Kiddush First cup of wine	קַדֵּשׁ
UR'CHATZ	We wash our hands	וּרְחַץ
KARPAS	We dip a vegetable in salt water and say a blessing	כַּרְפַּס
YACHATZ	We break the middle matzah and hide the larger piece, the Afikomen	יַחַץ
MAGGID	We tell the story of Passover Four Questions Second cup of wine	מַגִּיד
RACHTZAH	We wash our hands and say the blessing	רָחְצָה
MOTZI/ MATZAH	We say the blessings for "bread" and matzah	מוֹצִיא מַצָּה
MAROR	We dip the bitter herbs in charoset and say the blessing	מָרוֹר
KORECH	We eat a sandwich of matzah and bitter herbs	כּוֹרֵךְ
SHULCHAN ORECH	We eat the festive meal	שֻׁלְחָן עוֹרֵךְ
TZAFUN	We eat the Afikomen	צָפוּן
BARECH	We say the blessing after the meal Third cup of wine Welcome Elijah and Miriam	בָּרֵךְ
HALLEL	We sing songs of praise Fourth cup of wine	הַלֵּל
NIRTZAH	We complete the seder	נִרְצָה

The recitation or chanting of the parts of the seder emphasizes that the word *seder* means *order*. Just as a meeting has an agenda, so does the seder. As in meetings, we occasionally stray off the topic. Just remember to get back to the agenda . . . eventually.

Review the order of the seder. Everyone likes *shulchan orech* . . . the seder meal . . . but what other part(s) are you especially looking forward to this year? Why?

Share other places you have celebrated the Passover seder. Has anyone had an unusual experience?

קדש

WE SAY THE KIDDUSH

THE FIRST CUP

(Fill cups with wine or grape juice)

We lift our cups to say the blessing over the first cup of wine:

(On Shabbat, add the words in brackets)

[וַיְהִי־עֶרֶב וַיְהִי־בֹקֶר יוֹם הַשִּׁשִּׁי.
וַיְכֻלּוּ הַשָּׁמַיִם וְהָאָרֶץ וְכָל־צְבָאָם. וַיְכַל אֱלֹהִים בַּיּוֹם הַשְּׁבִיעִי מְלַאכְתּוֹ
אֲשֶׁר עָשָׂה, וַיִּשְׁבֹּת בַּיּוֹם הַשְּׁבִיעִי מִכָּל־מְלַאכְתּוֹ אֲשֶׁר עָשָׂה. וַיְבָרֶךְ
אֱלֹהִים אֶת־יוֹם הַשְּׁבִיעִי וַיְקַדֵּשׁ אֹתוֹ, כִּי בוֹ שָׁבַת מִכָּל־מְלַאכְתּוֹ אֲשֶׁר
בָּרָא אֱלֹהִים לַעֲשׂוֹת.]

[Vay'hi erev vay'hi voker yom hashishi. Vay'chulu hashamayim v'ha'aretz v'chol tz'va'am. Vay'chal Elohim bayom hash'vi'i m'lachto asher asah. Vayishbot bayom hash'vi'i mikol m'lachto asher asah. Vay'varech Elohim et yom hash'vi'i vay'kadesh oto, ki vo shavat mikol m'lachto asher bara Elohim la'asot.]

[On the sixth day, the heavens and the earth were completed. On the seventh day, God finished the work of creation and rested. God blessed the seventh day and called it holy, because on that day God rested from the work of creation.]

בָּרוּךְ אַתָּה יְיָ אֱלֹהֵינוּ מֶלֶךְ הָעוֹלָם בּוֹרֵא פְּרִי הַגָּפֶן.

Baruch Atah Adonai Eloheinu melech ha'olam, borei p'ri hagafen.

We praise You, Adonai our God, Ruler of the Universe, Who creates the fruit of the vine.

We drink four cups of wine at the seder to invoke the promises God made to the people Israel *(Exodus 6:6-7):*

I will bring you out . . .
I will deliver you . . .
I will redeem you . . .
I will take you to be my people . . .

Pesach celebrates freedom and redemption, yet it reminds us that we are neither truly free nor fully redeemed. While the Kiddush refers to the season of our "freedom," when we uncover the matzah we say, "Now we are slaves, next year may we be truly free." As the seder unfolds, notice how this tension is reflected at other moments.

בָּרוּךְ אַתָּה יְיָ אֱלֹהֵינוּ מֶלֶךְ הָעוֹלָם אֲשֶׁר בָּחַר בָּנוּ מִכָּל־עָם וְרוֹמְמָנוּ מִכָּל־לָשׁוֹן וְקִדְּשָׁנוּ בְּמִצְוֹתָיו. וַתִּתֶּן־לָנוּ יְיָ אֱלֹהֵינוּ בְּאַהֲבָה (שַׁבָּתוֹת לִמְנוּחָה וּ)מוֹעֲדִים לְשִׂמְחָה חַגִּים וּזְמַנִּים לְשָׂשׂוֹן אֶת־יוֹם (הַשַּׁבָּת הַזֶּה וְאֶת־יוֹם) חַג הַמַּצּוֹת הַזֶּה, זְמַן חֵרוּתֵנוּ, (בְּאַהֲבָה) מִקְרָא קֹדֶשׁ זֵכֶר לִיצִיאַת מִצְרָיִם. כִּי בָנוּ בָחַרְתָּ וְאוֹתָנוּ קִדַּשְׁתָּ מִכָּל־הָעַמִּים (וְשַׁבָּת) וּמוֹעֲדֵי קָדְשְׁךָ (בְּאַהֲבָה וּבְרָצוֹן) בְּשִׂמְחָה וּבְשָׂשׂוֹן הִנְחַלְתָּנוּ. בָּרוּךְ אַתָּה יְיָ מְקַדֵּשׁ (הַשַּׁבָּת וְ)יִשְׂרָאֵל וְהַזְּמַנִּים.

Baruch Atah Adonai Eloheinu melech ha'olam, asher bachar banu mikol am. V'rom'manu mikol lashon, v'kid'shanu b'mitzvotav. Vatiten lanu Adonai Eloheinu b'ahavah [Shabbatot lim'nuchah u'] mo'adim l'simchah chagim uz'manim l'sasson. Et yom [haShabbat hazeh v'et yom] chag hamatzot hazeh z'man cherutenu [b'ahavah] mikra kodesh zecher liy'tziat Mitzrayim. Ki vanu vacharta v'otanu kidashta mikol ha'amin [v'Shabbat] u'moadei kadsh'cha [b'ahavah] uv'ratzon b'simchah u'v'sasson hinchaltanu. Baruch Atah Adonai mikadesh [haShabbat v'] Yisrael v'hazmanim.

We praise You, Adonai our God, Ruler of the Universe, Who has made us holy through your mitzvot and lovingly given us [Shabbat for rest and] festivals for gladness. You have given us [Shabbat and] this Festival of Matzot, to celebrate our freedom, and to recall our going out of Egypt. We praise You Adonai, Who makes holy [Shabbat] the people Israel, and the festivals.

On Saturday night, add Havdallah (on facing page)

בָּרוּךְ אַתָּה יְיָ אֱלֹהֵינוּ מֶלֶךְ הָעוֹלָם שֶׁהֶחֱיָנוּ וְקִיְּמָנוּ וְהִגִּיעָנוּ לַזְּמַן הַזֶּה.

Baruch Atah Adonai, Eloheinu melech ha'olam shehecheyanu, v'kiy'manu, v'higianu, lazman hazeh.

We praise you, Adonai our God, Ruler of the Universe, Who has kept us alive and well so that we can celebrate this special time.

(All drink the wine or grape juice)

HAVDALLAH

בָּרוּךְ אַתָּה יְיָ אֱלֹהֵינוּ מֶלֶךְ הָעוֹלָם בּוֹרֵא
מְאוֹרֵי הָאֵשׁ.

Baruch Atah Adonai Eloheinu melech ha'olam, borei m'orei ha'esh.

We praise you, Adonai our God, Ruler of the Universe, Creator of light.

בָּרוּךְ אַתָּה יְיָ אֱלֹהֵינוּ מֶלֶךְ הָעוֹלָם הַמַּבְדִּיל
בֵּין קֹדֶשׁ לְחֹל, בֵּין אוֹר לְחֹשֶׁךְ, בֵּין יִשְׂרָאֵל
לָעַמִּים, בֵּין יוֹם הַשְּׁבִיעִי לְשֵׁשֶׁת יְמֵי הַמַּעֲשֶׂה.
בֵּין קְדֻשַּׁת שַׁבָּת לִקְדֻשַּׁת יוֹם טוֹב הִבְדַּלְתָּ,
וְאֶת־יוֹם הַשְּׁבִיעִי מִשֵּׁשֶׁת יְמֵי הַמַּעֲשֶׂה
קִדַּשְׁתָּ, הִבְדַּלְתָּ וְקִדַּשְׁתָּ אֶת־עַמְּךָ יִשְׂרָאֵל
בִּקְדֻשָּׁתֶךָ. בָּרוּךְ אַתָּה יְיָ הַמַּבְדִּיל בֵּין קֹדֶשׁ
לְקֹדֶשׁ.

Baruch Atah Adonai hamavdil bein kodesh l'kodesh.

We praise you Adonai our God, Ruler of the Universe, Who separates holy from not holy, light from darkness, Israel from the nations, and Shabbat from the six days of creation. We praise You, Adonai, Who separates the holiness of Shabbat from the holiness of the festivals.

Continue with Shehecheyanu (opposite)

The celebration of Pesach extends the spirit of Shabbat, so we do not recite the blessing over the spices. The blessing for light is said over the holiday candles and not over a Havdallah candle.

ורחץ WE WASH OUR HANDS

(Take a cup or pitcher of water in one hand and pour it over the other hand. Then do the same, reversing hands. This can be done at a sink, or with a cup and basin at the table. No blessing is recited.)

כרפס WE DIP A VEGETABLE

(Give everyone a green vegetable)

We dip a vegetable into salt water and say this blessing:

בָּרוּךְ אַתָּה יְיָ אֱלֹהֵינוּ מֶלֶךְ הָעוֹלָם בּוֹרֵא פְּרִי הָאֲדָמָה.

Baruch Atah Adonai Eloheinu melech ha'olam, borei p'ri ha'adamah.

We praise You, Adonai our God, Ruler of the Universe, Who creates the fruit of the earth.

(All eat the vegetable)

Before beginning their service in the Holy Temple in Jerusalem, the kohanim (priests) were commanded to wash their hands and feet. At the seder, the symbolic washing of hands reminds us that we are a "kingdom of priests and a holy nation," *(Exodus 19:8)* and our actions must be in service to God.[3]

DODI LI

The *Song of Songs*, which is read in synagogue on Passover, is both a beautiful love poem and an allegory of the relationship between God and the people Israel. For example, the verse, "I am my beloved's and my beloved is mine," can be viewed in both ways.

דּוֹדִי לִי וַאֲנִי לוֹ
הָרוֹעֶה בַּשּׁוֹשַׁנִּים.

מִי זֹאת עוֹלָה מִן הַמִּדְבָּר
מְקֻטֶּרֶת מוֹר וּלְבוֹנָה.

Dodi li va'ani lo, haro'eh bashoshanim.
Mi zot olah min hamidbar, m'kuteret mor ul'vonah?

My beloved is mine and I am his, who browses among the lilies. Who is she coming from the desert, in clouds of myrrh and frankincense?

Ask guests to bring or describe a sign of spring to share at the seder.

The Talmud suggests having a bowl of raisins and nuts for children (and adults!) to nosh during the seder. We can eat all kinds of nuts on Passover except peanuts, which are legumes like peas and beans, and not eaten by Ashkenazim on Passover.[4]

יחץ

WE BREAK THE MIDDLE MATZAH

We break the middle matzah into two pieces. We wrap and set aside the larger piece as the Afikomen, the dessert matzah to be eaten after the meal. The smaller piece is returned to its place.

(Uncover the plate of matzah and raise it for all to see)

הָא לַחְמָא עַנְיָא דִּי אֲכַלוּ אַבְהָתַנָא בְּאַרְעָא דְמִצְרָיִם. כָּל־דִּכְפִין יֵיתֵי וְיֵכֹל, כָּל־דִּצְרִיךְ יֵיתֵי וְיִפְסַח. הָשַׁתָּא הָכָא, לַשָּׁנָה הַבָּאָה בְּאַרְעָא דְיִשְׂרָאֵל. הָשַׁתָּא עַבְדֵי, לַשָּׁנָה הַבָּאָה בְּנֵי חוֹרִין.

Halachma Anya di achalu ahavatana b'ara d'Mitzrayim. Kol dichfin yeitei v'yechol. Kol ditzrich yetei v'yifsach. Hashata hacha lashanah haba'ah b'ara d'Yisrael. Hashata avdei lashanah haba'ah b'nei chorin.

This is the bread of poverty which our ancestors ate in the land of Egypt. All who are hungry, come and eat. All who are needy, come and celebrate Passover with us. Now we celebrate here. Next year may we be in the land of Israel. Now we are slaves. Next year may we be truly free.

(Fill the wine cups for the second time)

THE MATZAH OF HOPE

We set aside this matzah as a symbol of hope for all those in the world who are in despair. Some are crushed by poverty and disease, others by tyranny and violence. We pray that their pain will end soon, and they will be brought to safety and healing. We dedicate ourselves to relieve suffering in whatever form it takes.

No blessing is said when we break the middle matzah, because its brokenness is a symbol of incompleteness. It reminds us of all that needs repair *(tikkun)* in our world. Later we will taste a piece of the Afikomen, the larger portion of the middle matzah, again without reciting a blessing. This will affirm our belief that completeness will come in the future.[5]

Ha Lachma Anya ("this is the bread of affliction") is said in Aramaic, because the custom of inviting those who are hungry to the seder began in Babylonia, where the Jews spoke Aramaic.

We say "all who are hungry, come and eat" to teach us to share our food with others. We continue "all who are needy, come and celebrate" to teach us there are those with well-stocked pantries whose lives may be empty or lonely.

Based on this passage, there is a tradition of collecting funds to enable poor people to make their own seders. This custom is called *Ma'ot Chittin* (literally "wheat money"). Ask your local rabbi or educational director about charities that help feed the needy here and around the globe.

It has been suggested that we place an empty plate on our table to remember the homeless. They are even less fortunate than the Israelite slaves who, at least, had dwelling places.[6] Ask guests to "fill the plate" by pledging money or work hours at a shelter or soup kitchen.

מגיד

WE TELL THE STORY OF PASSOVER

THE FOUR QUESTIONS

מַה־נִּשְׁתַּנָּה הַלַּיְלָה הַזֶּה מִכָּל־הַלֵּילוֹת!

Mah nishtanah halailah hazeh mikol haleilot!

How different this night is from all other nights!

שֶׁבְּכָל־הַלֵּילוֹת אָנוּ אוֹכְלִין חָמֵץ וּמַצָּה,
הַלַּיְלָה הַזֶּה כֻּלּוֹ מַצָּה.

Sheb'chol haleilot anu ochlin chametz u'matzah.
Halailah hazeh kulo matzah.
On all other nights we eat bread or matzah.
On this night why do we eat only matzah?

שֶׁבְּכָל־הַלֵּילוֹת אָנוּ אוֹכְלִין שְׁאָר יְרָקוֹת,
הַלַּיְלָה הַזֶּה מָרוֹר.

Sheb'chol haleilot anu ochlin she'ar yirakot.
Halailah hazeh maror.
On all other nights we eat all kinds of vegetables.
On this night why do we eat only maror?

שֶׁבְּכָל־הַלֵּילוֹת אֵין אָנוּ מַטְבִּילִין אֲפִלּוּ פַּעַם אֶחָת,
הַלַּיְלָה הַזֶּה שְׁתֵּי פְעָמִים.

Sheb'chol haleilot ein anu matbilin afilu pa'am echat.
Halailah hazeh sh'tei f'amim.
On all other nights we do not have to dip vegetables even once.
On this night why do we dip them twice?

שֶׁבְּכָל־הַלֵּילוֹת אָנוּ אוֹכְלִין בֵּין יוֹשְׁבִין וּבֵין מְסֻבִּין,
הַלַּיְלָה הַזֶּה כֻּלָּנוּ מְסֻבִּין.

Sheb' chol haleilot anu ochlin bein yoshvin u'vein m'subin.
Halailah hazeh kulanu m'subin.
On all other nights we eat our meals sitting any way we like.
On this night, why do we lean on pillows?

The Maggid section of the Haggadah, which tells the story of Passover, begins with the Four Questions. This sets the tone for the rest of the seder. It suggests that we be active participants, responding with curiosity about the seder symbols as well as the text. The more we are involved, the more meaningful and memorable the seder will be.

In the original Haggadah text, one of the Four Questions referred to the Passover sacrifice (Talmud: *Pesachim 116a*). Since the destruction of the Temple in Jerusalem, we do not offer sacrifices. Therefore a question about reclining while eating was substituted.

Do you have a "fifth" question about the seder that you would like to ask?

Often, questions are raised but answers are lacking. Is it liberating to accept that not all questions can be answered?

If the youngest child is too shy to recite the Four Questions aloud, why not ask the oldest seder participant to join in?

WE BEGIN TO ANSWER

עֲבָדִים הָיִינוּ לְפַרְעֹה בְּמִצְרָיִם. וַיּוֹצִיאֵנוּ יְיָ אֱלֹהֵינוּ מִשָּׁם בְּיָד
חֲזָקָה וּבִזְרוֹעַ נְטוּיָה. וְאִלּוּ לֹא הוֹצִיא הַקָּדוֹשׁ בָּרוּךְ הוּא אֶת־
אֲבוֹתֵינוּ מִמִּצְרַיִם, הֲרֵי אָנוּ וּבָנֵינוּ וּבְנֵי בָנֵינוּ מְשֻׁעְבָּדִים הָיִינוּ
לְפַרְעֹה בְּמִצְרָיִם. וַאֲפִלּוּ כֻּלָּנוּ חֲכָמִים, כֻּלָּנוּ נְבוֹנִים, כֻּלָּנוּ
זְקֵנִים, כֻּלָּנוּ יוֹדְעִים אֶת־הַתּוֹרָה, מִצְוָה עָלֵינוּ לְסַפֵּר בִּיצִיאַת
מִצְרָיִם. וְכָל־הַמַּרְבֶּה לְסַפֵּר בִּיצִיאַת מִצְרַיִם הֲרֵי זֶה מְשֻׁבָּח.

Avadim hayinu l'Pharaoh b'Mitzrayim.

This night is different from all the other nights because once we were slaves to Pharaoh in Egypt, but Adonai, our God, took us out with a mighty hand and an outstretched arm. If Adonai had not brought our ancestors out of Egypt, then we, and our children, and our children's children would still be slaves in the land of Egypt. Even if we know the story well and have told it many times, the more we tell it in great detail, the more we are to be praised.

This night is also different because once we worshipped idols, but now we worship only Adonai, the One Who Is Everywhere.

בָּרוּךְ הַמָּקוֹם, בָּרוּךְ הוּא.
בָּרוּךְ שֶׁנָּתַן תּוֹרָה לְעַמּוֹ יִשְׂרָאֵל, בָּרוּךְ הוּא.

Baruch HaMakom, Baruch Hu.
Baruch shenatan Torah l'amo Yisrael, Baruch Hu.

Praised be God Who Is Everywhere. Praised be God.
Praised be God who gave the Torah to the people of Israel. Praised be God.

There is a tale in the Talmud about Rabbi Eliezer, Rabbi Yehoshua, Rabbi Elazar ben Azaria, Rabbi Akiba, and Rabbi Tarfon, who were gathered in B'nai B'rak discussing the Exodus from Egypt all through the night, until their students came to tell them: "Our teachers, the time has come to recite the morning *Sh'ma.*"

It has been suggested that these second-century scholars were not only discussing the Exodus, they were planning a rebellion against their Roman oppressors. How has the story of the Exodus inspired other revolutions?

Some say the students interrupted the rabbis to warn them that the Romans were coming. Others say they were signaling that the time for talking was over; they must act against the tyrant.

The story of these five sages is included in the Haggadah to serve as a model for us. Just as they deliberated long and hard, so we must not rush through the text, but should struggle with its meaning.

It is unusual for a people to tell its history by tracing its origins to slavery and degradation, but the Talmud says that when we tell the story of Pesach, we should begin with despair and end with joy. The Haggadah does this in two ways. First, we begin by telling how our people were slaves to Pharaoh in Egypt, and God brought them to freedom. Second, we relate that our ancestors were idol worshippers and now we worship only God.

THE FOUR CHILDREN

The Torah commands us to teach our children about Passover. The Talmud suggests four different ways children might react.

The WISE child might ask:

What is the meaning of the laws and rules which Adonai our God has commanded us?

We should explain to this child in great detail all the laws and customs of Passover.

The WICKED child might ask:

What does this service mean to you?

Since this child does not want to be included in the celebration, we must answer harshly: "We celebrate Passover because of what Adonai did for us. If you had been in Egypt, you would not have been included when Adonai freed us from slavery."

The SIMPLE child might ask:

What is this all about?

We answer simply that, "With a mighty hand Adonai took us out of Egypt."

What about the child who DOESN'T KNOW ENOUGH TO ASK A QUESTION?

We must explain to this child that we observe Passover to remember what God did for us when we were freed from slavery in Egypt.

Complete these sentences:

I am like the wise child when . . .
I am like the wicked child when . . .
I am like the simple child when . . .
I am like the child unable to ask when . . .

Do you agree with the Haggadah's answer to the wicked child? How would you answer?

Recently, it has been noted that missing from the list of children is the one who is unaware, apathetic, or disengaged. Who are these children (and adults) and how can they be brought to the seder table?

We remember another child, the child of the Holocaust who did not survive to ask questions. Therefore, we ask for that child…why? We can only answer with silence.[7]

THE STORY OF PASSOVER

Abraham, the first Jew, came from a family of idol worshippers. He broke with their tradition and became a believer in the One God, who promised him and his wife Sarah that their descendants would become a great people, as numerous as the stars in the sky. God renewed this promise with their son Isaac and his wife Rebecca, and with their son Jacob and his wives Rachel and Leah.

God led Abraham and Sarah across the river Euphrates to the land of Israel (then called Canaan), but warned that their descendants would be strangers in a strange land, enslaved for 400 years.

Indeed, this prophecy came true. Joseph, the son of Jacob and Rachel, came to live in Egypt after being sold by his jealous brothers to a caravan of merchants. Because of his ability to interpret dreams, he rose to power as an advisor to Pharaoh. Joseph told him to build storehouses and fill them with grain. When years of famine struck, there was still food to eat in Egypt. Pharaoh was so grateful that when Joseph's brothers came in search of food, he invited them to settle in the area called Goshen. Jacob's household, known as Israelites, multiplied greatly and lived peacefully in Egypt. Years later, a new Pharaoh came to rule, who did not remember Joseph and all he had done for the Egyptian people. He feared that the Israelites were becoming too numerous and too powerful and might side with the enemy if there should be war.

SLAVERY IN EGYPT

This Pharaoh made the Israelites slaves. He forced them to do hard labor, building cities with bricks made from clay and straw. The people knew neither peace nor rest, only misery and pain. The cruelest decree of all was Pharaoh's order that every baby boy born to an Israelite woman be drowned in the River Nile. The midwives, Shifra and Puah, feared God and did not do as the Pharaoh had ordered, but allowed the infants to live.

Most historians agree that the Pharaoh of the Passover story was Ramses II and the Exodus took place from 1280–1270 BCE.

The midwives, Shifra and Puah, did not kill the male babies at birth as commanded by Pharaoh. Instead, they risked the king's wrath, claiming that "the Hebrew women are not like the Egyptian women. They are vigorous. Before the midwife can come to them, they have given birth…" *(Exodus 1:19)*. When the midwives did this, they were breaking the law of the land. Are there circumstances today that justify breaking the law?

In your opinion, who is a modern Moses? A modern Aaron? A modern Miriam? A modern Pharaoh?

Although Moses was raised in Pharaoh's court, living a comfortable and privileged life, he felt a responsibility to help his people. In the Talmud *(Shavuot 39a)* it says: "All of Israel is responsible for one another." Do you agree?

Abraham Lincoln said: "As I would not be a slave, so I would not be a master," and "When one man is enslaved, no man is really free." How is someone who controls others not free? Where have we failed in achieving freedom?

In Chasidic teaching, the real slavery in Egypt was that the Hebrews had learned to endure it.

Seder go-round: In what ways are we presently slaves?

One couple, Amram and Yocheved, hid their newborn at home for three months. When his cries became too loud, Yocheved placed him in a basket on the river. Their daughter Miriam watched to see what would happen. When the Pharaoh's daughter came to bathe in the river, she discovered the basket. Feeling pity for the helpless child, she decided to keep him as her own and named him Moshe (Moses), meaning "drawn from the water."

Bravely, Miriam asked the princess if she needed a nurse to help her with the baby. The princess said yes, and so it happened that Yocheved was able to care for her own son and teach him about his heritage.

MOSES BECOMES A LEADER

Moses would have lived at the Pharaoh's palace forever, but he could not ignore the suffering of his people. Once, when he saw an Egyptian beating an Israelite slave, he was unable to control his anger, and he killed the Egyptian. Knowing his life would be in danger once the news of this deed spread, Moses fled to the land of Midian, where he became a shepherd.

One day, while tending sheep on Mount Horeb, Moses saw a bush that seemed to be on fire, but was not burning up. From the bush, he heard God's voice calling him. God said, "I am the God of your ancestors. I have seen the suffering of the Israelites and have heard their cries. I am ready to take them out of Egypt and bring them to a new land, a land flowing with milk and honey."

God told Moses to return to Egypt to bring the message of freedom to the Israelites, and to warn Pharaoh that God would bring plagues on the Egyptians if he did not let the slaves go free. Moses was so humble that he could not imagine being God's messenger. "I will be with you," God promised him. With this assurance and challenge, Moses set out for Egypt.

The Torah tells us that Moses was reluctant to be God's messenger. Do you see advantages for a hesitant leader versus an eager leader?

In many Haggadot there are no odes to Moses. Traditional texts do not even mention him. Some say this is so that we see the Exodus as the work of the Almighty and don't worship Moses as a god. Others say it is so we don't come to believe that we can only accomplish our goals when there is a strong leader. Each of us must act to bring freedom and peace.

MEET THE PRESS

Give out cards with names of Passover characters. Invite each character to "meet the press," as seder participants ask them probing questions about their role in the Passover story.[8]

SEDER TRIVIA

1. What instrument did Miriam use to lead the women in dance at the Sea of Reeds?

2. Why did God send locusts after the hail?

3. When did God say to Moses: "All the men who sought to kill you are dead."

4. Why did Pharaoh call the Israelites "shirkers?"

5. Why did Moses throw soot in the air in front of Pharaoh?

To find or check answers, see Exodus:
1) 15:20 2) 10:5 3) 4:19 4) 5:8, 5:17 5) 9:8-9

THE TEN PLAGUES

When Moses asked Pharaoh to free the Israelites, he refused, so God brought ten plagues on the Egyptians. Each one frightened Pharaoh, and each time he promised to free the slaves. But when each plague ended, Pharaoh did not keep his word. It was only after the last plague, the death of the firstborn of the Egyptians, that Pharaoh agreed to let the Israelites go.

We fill our wine cups to remember our joy in being able to leave Egypt. Yet our happiness is not complete, because the Egyptians, who are also God's children, suffered from Pharaoh's evil ways. Therefore, we spill a drop of wine from our cups (with a finger or a spoon) as we say each plague:

BLOOD	*Dahm*	דָּם
FROGS	*Tz'fardaya*	צְפַרְדֵּעַ
LICE	*Kinim*	כִּנִּים
BEASTS	*Arov*	עָרוֹב
CATTLE DISEASE	*Dever*	דֶּבֶר
BOILS	*Sh'chin*	שְׁחִין
HAIL	*Barad*	בָּרָד
LOCUSTS	*Arbeh*	אַרְבֶּה
DARKNESS	*Choshech*	חֹשֶׁךְ
PLAGUE OF THE FIRSTBORN	*Makat B'chorot*	מַכַּת בְּכוֹרוֹת

The plagues can be viewed as being "measure for measure" against Egypt. For example, the river is polluted because the Israelites were ordered to toss their newborn males into the sea. What other examples can you identify?

We note that the violence increases with each plague. Is this a model for revolution? Must we try nonviolent means first (pressure, strikes, boycotts) and use violence as a last resort?

Rabbi Arthur Waskow writes: "When a society acts idolatrous, when corporations act like Pharaoh by ignoring the common good in order to maximize their own power, nature itself rebels: the rivers turn to blood, frogs and vermin infest the earth, animals get sick, thick clouds of smoke blot out the sun and moon, ultimately human beings die. Indeed, the whole plague cycle in Exodus could be understood as a growing series of eco-disasters."[9] What do you think?

Seder go-round: What are some things that presently plague us?

CROSSING THE SEA

Soon after Pharaoh let the Israelites leave Egypt, he regretted his decision and ordered his army to bring them back. His soldiers caught up with the Israelites by the banks of the Sea of Reeds. When they saw the Egyptians, they were afraid and cried out. God told Moses to lift his staff. When he did, a strong east wind drove back the sea, leaving space for the Israelites to go across on dry land. The Egyptians came after them into the sea.

Moses again lifted his staff, and the waters rushed back, covering the Egyptians and their horses and chariots.

Then Moses' sister Miriam led the women in joyous dance and song, thanking God for saving their lives.

Thus Adonai our God brought us out of Egypt, not by an angel, nor by a seraph, nor by a messenger, but alone – with a mighty hand and an outstretched arm, and with great terror, and with signs and wonders.

GOD'S PROMISE

(Raise cup while saying)

וְהִיא שֶׁעָמְדָה לַאֲבוֹתֵינוּ וְלָנוּ. שֶׁלֹּא אֶחָד בִּלְבַד עָמַד עָלֵינוּ לְכַלּוֹתֵינוּ. אֶלָּא שֶׁבְּכָל־דּוֹר וָדוֹר עוֹמְדִים עָלֵינוּ לְכַלּוֹתֵינוּ. וְהַקָּדוֹשׁ בָּרוּךְ הוּא מַצִּילֵנוּ מִיָּדָם.

Vehi she'amdah la'avotenu v'lanu. Shelo echad bilvad amad aleinu l'chalotenu. Ela sheb'chol dor vador omdim aleinu l'chalotenu. VeHakadosh Baruch Hu matzilenu miyadam.

God promised Abraham that after 400 years of servitude, his descendants would leave the foreign land of their bondage and witness the judgment of their oppressors. It is this promise that has sustained the Jewish people in each generation, as enemies arose to destroy us. And the Holy One of Blessing saved us from their hand, enabling us to say, "Am Yisrael Chai," the Jewish people lives.

How do you view miracles in the Haggadah? As divine intervention? Well-timed natural phenomena? Parables? Visions? Dreams? What miracles have you experienced in your own life?

What signs of God's promise do you see today?

The Ten Commandments begins, "I am Adonai your God who brought you out of the land of Egypt, out of the house of bondage." Why is this the first thing God wants us to know?

DAYENU

Adonai has shown our people so many acts of kindness. For each one, we say, *dayenu*, meaning "that alone would have been enough, for that alone we are grateful."

אִלּוּ הוֹצִיאָנוּ מִמִּצְרַיִם, דַּיֵּנוּ.

Ilu hotzianu miMitzrayim. Dayenu.

אִלּוּ נָתַן לָנוּ אֶת־הַשַּׁבָּת, דַּיֵּנוּ.

Ilu natan lanu et haShabbat. Dayenu.

אִלּוּ נָתַן לָנוּ אֶת־הַתּוֹרָה, דַּיֵּנוּ.

Ilu natan lanu et haTorah. Dayenu.

Adonai took us out of Egypt	DAYENU
Punished the Egyptians and destroyed their idols	DAYENU
Divided the sea and led us across on dry land	DAYENU
Took care of us in the desert for forty years and fed us manna	DAYENU
Gave us Shabbat	DAYENU
Brought us to Mount Sinai and gave us the Torah	DAYENU
Brought us to the land of Israel and built the Holy Temple	DAYENU
For all these—alone and together—we say	DAYENU!

Dayenu teaches us to switch from the mentality of always wanting more to being grateful for what we have.

Of all the deeds that God performed for the Jewish people, for which are you the most grateful?

What are your personal dayenus?

THE PASSOVER SYMBOLS

Rabbi Gamliel said that in telling the story of the Exodus, we must explain the meaning of the three most important symbols. Without this explanation our celebration is incomplete.

PESACH 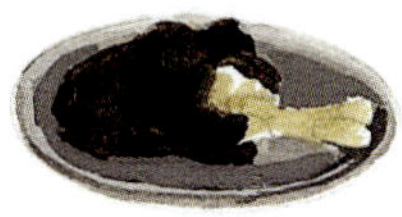 פסח

(Point to the lamb bone or beet)

The roasted bone is called the Pesach (Passover). It recalls the lamb our ancestors sacrificed and ate in the days of the Temple. As a symbol on our seder plate, it reminds us that during the tenth plague, Adonai "passed over" the homes of the Israelites and spared their first born.

MATZAH  מצה

(Lift up the matzah)

We eat matzah to remind us how our ancestors had to leave Egypt in such haste that the dough for their bread did not have time to rise.

MAROR  מרור

(Lift up the bitter herb)

We eat this maror to remind us how bitter the Egyptians made the lives of our ancestors by forcing them to be slaves.

MATZAH FACTS

• Matzah has holes to keep it from rising.

• *Shemurah* (guarded) matzah is carefully watched from the time the wheat is cut until the matzah is finally baked, so that no moisture causes it to become *chametz* (leavened).

• To make matzah we must work the dough for no longer than 18 minutes or else the natural process of fermentation, or leavening, will occur.

• Matzah is a metaphor for our own lives. It teaches us that if we want to achieve freedom, we cannot just sit back and let nature take its course.[10]

• Matzah is both the bread of slavery and the bread of freedom. It is the only Passover symbol with two opposing meanings. Reb Nachman of Bratslov taught that the bread itself did not change, but its taste did.[11]

A roasted egg placed on the seder plate commemorates the Passover offering brought to the Temple in Jerusalem. It is also a symbol of renewal that proclaims our hope for future redemption.

In some Sephardic households, the egg is eaten by a first born as a sign of gratitude to God for sparing the Israelite first born during the tenth plague.[12]

Seder go-round: What other food would you choose as a Passover symbol? Why?

IN EVERY GENERATION

בְּכָל־דּוֹר וָדוֹר חַיָּב אָדָם לִרְאוֹת אֶת־עַצְמוֹ כְּאִלּוּ הוּא יָצָא מִמִּצְרַיִם.

B'chol dor vador chayav adam lirot et atzmo k'ilo hu yatza mi'Mitzrayim.

In each generation, everyone must think of himself or herself as having personally left Egypt.

SONGS OF PRAISE

(Lift wine cups and say)

It is our duty to give thanks, sing praises, and offer blessings to the Holy One Who did these miracles for our ancestors and for us. For bringing us:

from slavery to freedom,
from sadness to joy,
from darkness to light.

וְנֹאמַר לְפָנָיו שִׁירָה חֲדָשָׁה, הַלְלוּיָהּ.

Venomar l'fanav shirah chadashah, Halleluyah.

Therefore, let us sing a new song, Halleluyah.

הַלְלוּיָהּ. הַלְלוּ עַבְדֵי יְיָ,
הַלְלוּ אֶת־שֵׁם יְיָ.
יְהִי שֵׁם יְיָ מְבֹרָךְ
מֵעַתָּה וְעַד עוֹלָם.

Halleluyah hal'lu avdei Adonai,
Hallelu et shem Adonai.
Yehi shem Adonai m'vorach
Me'atah v'ad olam.

Halleluyah.
Give praise to Adonai.
Sing praises, those who serve Adonai.
Blessed is the Name of Adonai now and forever.

Our seder goal is to relate personally to the Passover story. What stories in your family's history need to be told?

Spend a few minutes imagining you are in Egypt. What do you see . . . hear . . . feel?

In our own generation it is said that each Jew is a "Jew by choice." What are your reasons for being Jewish in a world of choice?

בְּצֵאת יִשְׂרָאֵל מִמִּצְרָיִם בֵּית יַעֲקֹב מֵעַם לֹעֵז.
הָיְתָה יְהוּדָה לְקָדְשׁוֹ יִשְׂרָאֵל מַמְשְׁלוֹתָיו.
הַיָּם רָאָה וַיָּנֹס הַיַּרְדֵּן יִסֹּב לְאָחוֹר.
הֶהָרִים רָקְדוּ כְאֵילִים גְּבָעוֹת כִּבְנֵי־צֹאן.
מַה־לְּךָ הַיָּם, כִּי תָנוּס הַיַּרְדֵּן תִּסֹּב לְאָחוֹר
הֶהָרִים תִּרְקְדוּ כְאֵילִים גְּבָעוֹת, כִּבְנֵי־צֹאן
מִלִּפְנֵי אָדוֹן חוּלִי אָרֶץ מִלִּפְנֵי אֱלוֹהַּ יַעֲקֹב.
הַהֹפְכִי הַצּוּר אֲגַם־מָיִם חַלָּמִישׁ לְמַעְיְנוֹ־מָיִם.

When the people of Israel left Egypt, they became God's people. The sea fled at the sight, and the river Jordan turned backwards. Mountains skipped like rams, and all of nature trembled at the presence of the Holy One.

THE SECOND CUP

(Lift wine cups and say)

We praise You, Adonai our God, Ruler of the Universe, Who has freed us and our ancestors from Egypt and brought us here this night to eat matzah and maror. Adonai, our God and God of our ancestors, help us celebrate future holidays and festivals in peace and in joy. Then we will thank You with a new song.

בָּרוּךְ אַתָּה יְיָ גָּאַל יִשְׂרָאֵל.

Baruch Atah Adonai, ga'al Yisrael.

We praise You, Adonai our God, Who has freed the people of Israel.

בָּרוּךְ אַתָּה יְיָ, אֱלֹהֵינוּ מֶלֶךְ הָעוֹלָם בּוֹרֵא פְּרִי הַגָּפֶן.

Baruch Atah Adonai Eloheinu melech ha'olam, borei p'ri hagafen.

We praise You, Adonai our God, Ruler of the Universe, Who creates the fruit of the vine.

(Drink the second cup)

B'TZET YISRAEL

B'tzet Yisrael mi'Mitzrayim;
Bet Ya'akov me'am lo'ez.
Hay'tah Yehudah l'kadsho;
Yisrael mamsh'lotav.
Hayam ra'ah vayanos;
HaYarden yisov l'achor.
Heharim rakdu ch'eilim;
G'va'ot kiv'nei tzon.
Mah l'cha hayam ki tanus;
HaYarden tisov l'achor.
Heharim tirk'du ch'eilim;
G'vaot kiv'nei tzon.
Milifnei adon chuli aretz;
Milifnei Elohai Ya'akov.
Hahofchi hatzur agam mayim;
Chalamish l'maiy'no mayim.

רחצה
WE WASH OUR HANDS

We wash our hands for the meal and say this blessing:

בָּרוּךְ אַתָּה יְיָ אֱלֹהֵינוּ מֶלֶךְ הָעוֹלָם אֲשֶׁר קִדְּשָׁנוּ בְּמִצְוֹתָיו
וְצִוָּנוּ עַל נְטִילַת יָדָיִם.

Baruch Atah Adonai Eloheinu Melech ha'olam, asher kid'shanu b'mitzvotav v'tzivanu al n'tilat yadayim.

We praise You, Adonai our God, Ruler of the Universe, Who has made us holy by Your mitzvot and commands us to wash our hands.

מוציא מצה
WE SAY BLESSINGS FOR MATZAH

(Distribute pieces of the upper and middle matzah)

בָּרוּךְ אַתָּה יְיָ אֱלֹהֵינוּ מֶלֶךְ הָעוֹלָם הַמּוֹצִיא לֶחֶם מִן הָאָרֶץ.

Baruch Atah Adonai Eloheinu melech ha'olam, hamotzi lechem min ha'aretz.

We praise You, Adonai our God, Ruler of the Universe, Who brings forth bread from the earth.

בָּרוּךְ אַתָּה יְיָ אֱלֹהֵינוּ מֶלֶךְ הָעוֹלָם אֲשֶׁר קִדְּשָׁנוּ בְּמִצְוֹתָיו
וְצִוָּנוּ עַל אֲכִילַת מַצָּה.

Baruch Atah Adonai Eloheinu melech ha'olam, asher kid'shanu b'mitzvotav v'tzivanu al achilat matzah.

We praise You, Adonai our God, Ruler of the Universe, Who makes us holy by Your mitzvot and commands us to eat matzah.

(Eat the matzah)

At a seder in the concentration camp of Bergen-Belsen, Rabbi Israel Spira of Bluzhov taught: "Life contains moments of bread (creativity and light) and moments of matzah (suffering and despair). But on this night of great humiliation and degradation, there is only matzah." He went on to assure, especially the children, that they should not despair, for it was the beginning of the redemption. "At the end of the long night in the land of the shadow of death, there would shine a great light, as our prophets promised."[14]

Let us pause to remember all who suffered and all who perished in the Holocaust, and in their honor and in their memory commit ourselves to oppose discrimination and genocide wherever they may take place.

מָרוֹר WE SAY THE BLESSING FOR MAROR

(Give everyone a piece of maror and some charoset)

We dip the maror into charoset to recall that our ancestors were able to withstand the bitterness of slavery, because it was sweetened by the hope of freedom.

בָּרוּךְ אַתָּה יְיָ אֱלֹהֵינוּ מֶלֶךְ הָעוֹלָם אֲשֶׁר קִדְּשָׁנוּ בְּמִצְוֹתָיו וְצִוָּנוּ עַל אֲכִילַת מָרוֹר.

Baruch Atah Adonai Eloheinu melech ha'olam, asher kid'shanu b'mitzvotav v'tzivanu al achilat maror.

We praise You, Adonai our God, Ruler of the Universe, Who makes us holy by Your mitzvot and commands us to eat maror.

(Eat the maror and charoset)

כּוֹרֵךְ WE EAT A SANDWICH OF MATZAH AND MAROR

(Distribute pieces of maror and the bottom matzah)

On Passover, in the days of the Temple in Jerusalem, Rabbi Hillel would eat a sandwich made of the Pesach (lamb offering), matzah, and maror. Now we do not bring sacrifices to the Temple, so our sandwich is made only with matzah and maror.

(Eat the Hillel sandwich)

שֻׁלְחָן עוֹרֵךְ WE EAT THE FESTIVE MEAL

Many families traditionally serve hard-boiled eggs at the beginning of the meal, perhaps because they are a symbol of spring and renewal. They also remind us of the brave Jewish midwives who refused to carry out Pharaoh's order to kill male babies, and thus assured Jewish survival.

Why do we praise God for having us eat bitter herbs?

Some seder plates include an additional bitter food called *hazeret*. Lettuce (usually romaine) is used for the hazeret because it tastes sweet at first but then turns bitter. The Jerusalem Talmud *(Pesachim 29b)* compares this to the fact that the Egyptians were at first kind to the Israelites, but later embittered their lives. The lettuce is used for the Hillel sandwich, eaten to fulfill the saying: "With matzah and maror, they shall eat (the Pascal lamb)."

צָפוּן

WE EAT THE AFIKOMEN

After the afikomen has been found or ransomed, everyone gets a piece to eat. The afikomen is shared just as the Pesach offering was shared in the days of the Temple, to show that we are all responsible for one another. No special blessing is said because the dessert is part of the meal. We are not permitted to eat anything after the afikomen. Its taste should linger in our mouths.

בָּרֵךְ

WE SAY THE BLESSING AFTER THE MEAL

(Pour the third cup of wine and say)

בָּרוּךְ אַתָּה יְיָ אֱלֹהֵינוּ מֶלֶךְ הָעוֹלָם, הַזָּן אֶת־הָעוֹלָם כֻּלּוֹ בְּטוּבוֹ, בְּחֵן בְּחֶסֶד וּבְרַחֲמִים. הוּא נוֹתֵן לֶחֶם לְכָל־בָּשָׂר כִּי לְעוֹלָם חַסְדּוֹ. וּבְטוּבוֹ הַגָּדוֹל תָּמִיד לֹא חָסַר לָנוּ, וְאַל יֶחְסַר־לָנוּ מָזוֹן לְעוֹלָם וָעֶד בַּעֲבוּר שְׁמוֹ הַגָּדוֹל, כִּי הוּא זָן וּמְפַרְנֵס לַכֹּל וּמֵטִיב לַכֹּל וּמֵכִין מָזוֹן לְכָל־בְּרִיּוֹתָיו אֲשֶׁר בָּרָא. בָּרוּךְ אַתָּה יְיָ הַזָּן אֶת־הַכֹּל.

עֹשֶׂה שָׁלוֹם בִּמְרוֹמָיו הוּא יַעֲשֶׂה שָׁלוֹם עָלֵינוּ וְעַל כָּל־יִשְׂרָאֵל וְאִמְרוּ אָמֵן.

We praise You, Adonai our God, Ruler of the Universe, Who in goodness, mercy, and kindness gives food to the world. Your love for us endures forever. We praise You, Adonai, Who provides food for all life.

May the Holy One, Who makes peace in the Heavens, make peace for us, for Israel, and for all the world.

Before eating the Afikomen, invite children (and adults!) outside to jump rope. It provides a needed stretch and has symbolic meaning. The rope, which recalls the whip that the Egyptian taskmaster used to drive the Hebrew slaves, has been turned from an instrument of torture into a plaything.[15]

Which is better . . . for children to hide the afikomen and seek a ransom for its return, or to have a seder leader hide it and reward whoever finds it? Divide into teams for a lively debate.

In Iraq, the father asks the youngest child, "Are you willing to guard the afikomen? If you lose it, you will have to pay 1000 gold pieces." When s/he agrees, the afikomen is tied to his or her body in a special cloth, and everyone tries to talk the child into giving it away.[16]

In Morocco, it is a custom for each guest to take a piece of the afikomen and carry it as a protection against evil.[17]

BIRKAT HAMAZON

Baruch Atah Adonai Eloheinu melech ha'olam, hazan et ha'olam kulo b'tuvo b'chen b'chesed uv'rachamim. Hu noten lechem l'chol basar ki l'olam chasdo. Uv'tuvo hagadol tamid lo chasar lanu v'al yech'sar lanu mazon l'olam va'ed. Ba'avur sh'mo hagadol ki hu zan um'farnes lakol umetiv lakol umechin mazon l'chol b'riyotav asher bara. Baruch Atah Adonai hazan et hakol.

Oseh shalom bimromov Hu ya'aseh shalom aleinu v'al kol Yisrael v'imru amen.

(The full Birkat Hamazon is on the next two pages)

שִׁיר הַמַּעֲלוֹת. בְּשׁוּב יְיָ אֶת שִׁיבַת צִיּוֹן הָיִינוּ כְּחֹלְמִים. אָז יִמָּלֵא שְׂחוֹק פִּינוּ וּלְשׁוֹנֵנוּ רִנָּה. אָז יֹאמְרוּ בַגּוֹיִם הִגְדִּיל יְיָ לַעֲשׂוֹת עִם אֵלֶּה. הִגְדִּיל יְיָ לַעֲשׂוֹת עִמָּנוּ, הָיִינוּ שְׂמֵחִים.שׁוּבָה יְיָ אֶת שְׁבִיתֵנוּ כַּאֲפִיקִים בַּנֶּגֶב. הַזֹּרְעִים בְּדִמְעָה בְּרִנָּה יִקְצֹרוּ. הָלוֹךְ יֵלֵךְ וּבָכֹה נֹשֵׂא מֶשֶׁךְ הַזָּרַע, בֹּא יָבֹא בְרִנָּה נֹשֵׂא אֲלֻמֹּתָיו.

Leader:

רַבּוֹתַי נְבָרֵךְ.

Participants, then leader:

יְהִי שֵׁם יְיָ מְבֹרָךְ מֵעַתָּה וְעַד עוֹלָם.

Leader:

בִּרְשׁוּת רַבֹּתַי נְבָרֵךְ (אֱלֹהֵינוּ) שֶׁאָכַלְנוּ מִשֶּׁלּוֹ.

Participants, then leader:

בָּרוּךְ (אֱלֹהֵינוּ) שֶׁאָכַלְנוּ מִשֶּׁלּוֹ וּבְטוּבוֹ חָיִינוּ.

All:

בָּרוּךְ הוּא וּבָרוּךְ שְׁמוֹ.

בָּרוּךְ אַתָּה יְיָ אֱלֹהֵינוּ מֶלֶךְ הָעוֹלָם, הַזָּן אֶת הָעוֹלָם כֻּלּוֹ בְּטוּבוֹ, בְּחֵן בְּחֶסֶד וּבְרַחֲמִים.הוּא נוֹתֵן לֶחֶם לְכָל בָּשָׂר, כִּי לְעוֹלָם חַסְדּוֹ.וּבְטוּבוֹ הַגָּדוֹל תָּמִיד לֹא חָסַר לָנוּ, וְאַל יֶחְסַר לָנוּ מָזוֹן לְעוֹלָם וָעֶד בַּעֲבוּר שְׁמוֹ הַגָּדוֹל כִּי הוּא זָן וּמְפַרְנֵס לַכֹּל, וּמֵטִיב לַכֹּל, וּמֵכִין מָזוֹן לְכָל בְּרִיּוֹתָיו אֲשֶׁר בָּרָא. בָּרוּךְ אַתָּה יְיָ הַזָּן אֶת הַכֹּל.

נוֹדֶה לְךָ יְיָ אֱלֹהֵינוּ עַל שֶׁהִנְחַלְתָּ לַאֲבוֹתֵינוּ אֶרֶץ חֶמְדָּה טוֹבָה וּרְחָבָה; וְעַל שֶׁהוֹצֵאתָנוּ, יְיָ אֱלֹהֵינוּ מֵאֶרֶץ מִצְרַיִם, וּפְדִיתָנוּ מִבֵּית עֲבָדִים, וְעַל בְּרִיתְךָ שֶׁחָתַמְתָּ בִּבְשָׂרֵנוּ, וְעַל תּוֹרָתְךָ שֶׁלִּמַּדְתָּנוּ, וְעַל חֻקֶּיךָ שֶׁהוֹדַעְתָּנוּ, וְעַל חַיִּים חֵן וָחֶסֶד שֶׁחוֹנַנְתָּנוּ, וְעַל אֲכִילַת מָזוֹן שָׁאַתָּה זָן וּמְפַרְנֵס אוֹתָנוּ תָּמִיד, בְּכָל יוֹם וּבְכָל עֵת וּבְכָל שָׁעָה.

וְעַל הַכֹּל יְיָ אֱלֹהֵינוּ אֲנַחְנוּ מוֹדִים לָךְ וּמְבָרְכִים אוֹתָךְ; יִתְבָּרַךְ שִׁמְךָ בְּפִי כָּל חַי תָּמִיד לְעוֹלָם וָעֶד, כַּכָּתוּב: וְאָכַלְתָּ וְשָׂבָעְתָּ, וּבֵרַכְתָּ אֶת יְיָ אֱלֹהֶיךָ עַל הָאָרֶץ הַטּוֹבָה אֲשֶׁר נָתַן לָךְ. בָּרוּךְ אַתָּה יְיָ, עַל הָאָרֶץ וְעַל הַמָּזוֹן.

רַחֵם יְיָ אֱלֹהֵינוּ עַל יִשְׂרָאֵל עַמֶּךָ, וְעַל יְרוּשָׁלַיִם עִירֶךָ, וְעַל צִיּוֹן מִשְׁכַּן כְּבוֹדֶךָ, וְעַל מַלְכוּת בֵּית דָּוִד מְשִׁיחֶךָ, וְעַל הַבַּיִת הַגָּדוֹל וְהַקָּדוֹשׁ שֶׁנִּקְרָא שִׁמְךָ עָלָיו.אֱלֹהֵינוּ אָבִינוּ,רְעֵנוּ זוּנֵנוּ, פַּרְנְסֵנוּ וְכַלְכְּלֵנוּ וְהַרְוִיחֵנוּ וְהַרְוַח לָנוּ יְיָ אֱלֹהֵינוּ מְהֵרָה מִכָּל צָרוֹתֵינוּ. וְנָא אַל תַּצְרִיכֵנוּ יְיָ אֱלֹהֵינוּ לֹא לִידֵי מַתְּנַת בָּשָׂר וָדָם וְלֹא לִידֵי הַלְוָאָתָם, כִּי אִם לְיָדְךָ הַמְּלֵאָה הַפְּתוּחָה, הַקְּדוֹשָׁה וְהָרְחָבָה, שֶׁלֹּא נֵבוֹשׁ וְלֹא נִכָּלֵם לְעוֹלָם וָעֶד.

On Shabbat:

רְצֵה וְהַחֲלִיצֵנוּ יְיָ אֱלֹהֵינוּ בְּמִצְוֹתֶיךָ וּבְמִצְוַת יוֹם הַשְּׁבִיעִי, הַשַּׁבָּת הַגָּדוֹל וְהַקָּדוֹשׁ הַזֶּה כִּי יוֹם זֶה גָּדוֹל וְקָדוֹשׁ הוּא לְפָנֶיךָ, לִשְׁבָּת בּוֹ וְלָנוּחַ בּוֹ בְּאַהֲבָה כְּמִצְוַת רְצוֹנֶךָ. וּבִרְצוֹנְךָ הָנַח לָנוּ יְיָ אֱלֹהֵינוּ שֶׁלֹּא תְהִי צָרָה, וְיָגוֹן וַאֲנָחָה בְּיוֹם מְנוּחָתֵנוּ. וְהַרְאֵנוּ יְיָ אֱלֹהֵינוּ בְּנֶחָמַת צִיּוֹן עִירֶךָ, וּבְבִנְיַן יְרוּשָׁלַיִם עִיר קָדְשֶׁךָ, כִּי אַתָּה הוּא בַּעַל הַיְשׁוּעוֹת וּבַעַל הַנֶּחָמוֹת.

אֱלֹהֵינוּ וֵאלֹהֵי אֲבוֹתֵינוּ (וְאִמּוֹתֵינוּ), יַעֲלֶה וְיָבֹא, וְיַגִּיעַ , וְיֵרָאֶה, וְיֵרָצֶה וְיִשָּׁמַע, וְיִפָּקֵד וְיִזָּכֵר זִכְרוֹנֵנוּ וּפִקְדּוֹנֵנוּ, וְזִכְרוֹן אֲבוֹתֵינוּ, וְזִכְרוֹן מָשִׁיחַ בֶּן דָּוִד עַבְדֶּךָ, וְזִכְרוֹן יְרוּשָׁלַיִם עִיר קָדְשֶׁךָ,וְזִכְרוֹן כָּל עַמְּךָ בֵּית יִשְׂרָאֵל לְפָנֶיךָ, לִפְלֵיטָה

וּלְטוֹבָה, לְחֵן וּלְחֶסֶד וּלְרַחֲמִים, לְחַיִּים וּלְשָׁלוֹם בְּיוֹם חַג הַמַּצּוֹת הַזֶּה. זָכְרֵנוּ יְיָ אֱלֹהֵינוּ בּוֹ לְטוֹבָה, וּפָקְדֵנוּ בוֹ לִבְרָכָה,וְהוֹשִׁיעֵנוּ בוֹ לְחַיִּים. וּבִדְבַר יְשׁוּעָה וְרַחֲמִים חוּס וְחָנֵּנוּ, וְרַחֵם עָלֵינוּ וְהוֹשִׁיעֵנוּ כִּי אֵלֶיךָ עֵינֵינוּ, כִּי אֵל מֶלֶךְ חַנּוּן וְרַחוּם אָתָּה.

וּבְנֵי יְרוּשָׁלַיִם עִיר הַקּוֹדֶשׁ בִּמְהֵרָה בְיָמֵינוּ. בָּרוּךְ אַתָּה יְיָ, בּוֹנֶה בְרַחֲמָיו יְרוּשָׁלַיִם, אָמֵן.

בָּרוּךְ אַתָּה יְיָ אֱלֹהֵינוּ מֶלֶךְ הָעוֹלָם, הָאֵל אָבִינוּ מַלְכֵּנוּ אַדִּירֵנוּ בּוֹרְאֵנוּ גּוֹאֲלֵנוּ יוֹצְרֵנוּ קְדוֹשֵׁנוּ קְדוֹשׁ יַעֲקֹב, רוֹעֵנוּ רוֹעֵה יִשְׂרָאֵל, הַמֶּלֶךְ הַטּוֹב וְהַמֵּטִיב לַכֹּל, שֶׁבְּכָל יוֹם וָיוֹם הוּא הֵטִיב, הוּא מֵטִיב, הוּא יֵיטִיב לָנוּ. הוּא גְמָלָנוּ, הוּא גוֹמְלֵנוּ, הוּא יִגְמְלֵנוּ לָעַד, לְחֵן לְחֶסֶד וּלְרַחֲמִים וּלְרֶוַח הַצָּלָה וְהַצְלָחָה, בְּרָכָה וִישׁוּעָה נֶחָמָה פַּרְנָסָה וְכַלְכָּלָה, וְרַחֲמִים וְחַיִּים וְשָׁלוֹם וְכָל טוֹב, וּמִכָּל טוּב לְעוֹלָם אַל יְחַסְּרֵנוּ.

הָרַחֲמָן, הוּא יִמְלוֹךְ עָלֵינוּ לְעוֹלָם וָעֶד.

הָרַחֲמָן, הוּא יִתְבָּרַךְ בַּשָּׁמַיִם וּבָאָרֶץ.

הָרַחֲמָן, הוּא יִשְׁתַּבַּח לְדוֹר דּוֹרִים, וְיִתְפָּאַר בָּנוּ לָעַד וּלְנֵצַח נְצָחִים, וְיִתְהַדַּר בָּנוּ לָעַד וּלְעוֹלְמֵי עוֹלָמִים.

הָרַחֲמָן, הוּא יְפַרְנְסֵנוּ בְּכָבוֹד.

הָרַחֲמָן, הוּא יִשְׁבּוֹר עֻלֵּנוּ מֵעַל צַוָּארֵנוּ, וְהוּא יוֹלִיכֵנוּ קוֹמְמִיּוּת לְאַרְצֵנוּ.

הָרַחֲמָן, הוּא יִשְׁלַח בְּרָכָה מְרֻבָּה בַּבַּיִת הַזֶּה, וְעַל שֻׁלְחָן זֶה שֶׁאָכַלְנוּ עָלָיו.

הָרַחֲמָן, הוּא יִשְׁלַח לָנוּ אֶת אֵלִיָּהוּ הַנָּבִיא, זָכוּר לַטּוֹב, וִיבַשֶּׂר לָנוּ בְּשׂוֹרוֹת טוֹבוֹת,יְשׁוּעוֹת וְנֶחָמוֹת.

הָרַחֲמָן, הוּא יְבָרֵךְ אֶת כָּל הַמְּסֻבִּים כַּאן, אוֹתָנוּ וְאֶת כָּל אֲשֶׁר לָנוּ, כְּמוֹ שֶׁנִּתְבָּרְכוּ אֲבוֹתֵינוּ אַבְרָהָם יִצְחָק וְיַעֲקֹב (וְאִמּוֹתֵינוּ שָׂרָה, רִבְקָה, רָחֵל, וְלֵאָה) בַּכֹּל, מִכֹּל, כֹּל. כֵּן יְבָרֵךְ אוֹתָנוּ כֻּלָּנוּ יַחַד בִּבְרָכָה שְׁלֵמָה,וְנֹאמַר אָמֵן.

בַּמָּרוֹם יְלַמְּדוּ עֲלֵיהֶם וְעָלֵינוּ זְכוּת שֶׁתְּהֵי לְמִשְׁמֶרֶת שָׁלוֹם. וְנִשָּׂא בְרָכָה מֵאֵת יְיָ וּצְדָקָה מֵאֱלֹהֵי יִשְׁעֵנוּ. וְנִמְצָא חֵן וְשֵׂכֶל טוֹב בְּעֵינֵי אֱלֹהִים וְאָדָם.

On Shabbat:

הָרַחֲמָן, הוּא יַנְחִילֵנוּ יוֹם שֶׁכֻּלּוֹ שַׁבָּת וּמְנוּחָה לְחַיֵּי הָעוֹלָמִים.

הָרַחֲמָן, הוּא יַנְחִילֵנוּ יוֹם שֶׁכֻּלּוֹ טוֹב.

הָרַחֲמָן, הוּא יְזַכֵּנוּ לִימוֹת הַמָּשִׁיחַ וּלְחַיֵּי הָעוֹלָם הַבָּא.

מִגְדּוֹל יְשׁוּעוֹת מַלְכּוֹ וְעֹשֶׂה חֶסֶד לִמְשִׁיחוֹ, לְדָוִד וּלְזַרְעוֹ עַד עוֹלָם. עֹשֶׂה שָׁלוֹם בִּמְרוֹמָיו, הוּא יַעֲשֶׂה שָׁלוֹם עָלֵינוּ וְעַל כָּל יִשְׂרָאֵל, וְאִמְרוּ אָמֵן.

יְראוּ אֶת יְיָ קְדֹשָׁיו, כִּי אֵין מַחְסוֹר לִירֵאָיו. כְּפִירִים רָשׁוּ וְרָעֵבוּ וְדֹרְשֵׁי יְיָ לֹא יַחְסְרוּ כָל טוֹב. הוֹדוּ לַייָ כִּי טוֹב, כִּי לְעוֹלָם חַסְדּוֹ. פּוֹתֵחַ אֶת יָדֶךָ, וּמַשְׂבִּיעַ לְכָל חַי רָצוֹן.בָּרוּךְ הַגֶּבֶר אֲשֶׁר יִבְטַח בַּייָ, וְהָיָה יְיָ מִבְטַחוֹ. נַעַר הָיִיתִי גַּם זָקַנְתִּי וְלֹא רָאִיתִי צַדִּיק נֶעֱזָב וְזַרְעוֹ מְבַקֶּשׁ לָחֶם. יְיָ עֹז לְעַמּוֹ יִתֵּן יְיָ יְבָרֵךְ אֶת עַמּוֹ בַשָּׁלוֹם.

THE THIRD CUP

(Lift wine cups and say)

בָּרוּךְ אַתָּה יְיָ אֱלֹהֵינוּ מֶלֶךְ הָעוֹלָם בּוֹרֵא פְּרִי הַגָּפֶן.

Baruch Atah Adonai Eloheinu melech ha'olam, borei p'ri hagafen.

We praise You, Adonai our God, Ruler of the Universe, Who creates the fruit of the vine.

(Drink the wine)

WELCOMING ELIJAH

(Pour a cup of wine and put it in the center of the table)

This cup is for Eliyahu Hanavi, Elijah the Prophet. We open our front door to greet our honored guest and invite him to join our seder. We pray that he will return to us bringing a time of peace and freedom.

אֵלִיָּהוּ הַנָּבִיא, אֵלִיָּהוּ הַתִּשְׁבִּי,
אֵלִיָּהוּ, אֵלִיָּהוּ, אֵלִיָּהוּ הַגִּלְעָדִי,
בִּמְהֵרָה בְיָמֵינוּ יָבֹא אֵלֵינוּ עִם מָשִׁיחַ בֶּן דָּוִד.

Eliyahu hanavi, Eliyahu haTishbi,
Eliyahu, Eliyahu, Eliyahu haGiladi,
Bimhera v'yameinu, yavo eleinu im Mashiach ben David.

May Elijah the Prophet come to us quickly and in our day, bringing the time of the Messiah.

Pesach eve was also called "the Night of Watching." The door was left open as if participants were ready to leave at a moment's notice. When it became dangerous to keep doors open, the practice changed. Now we remember this night by opening the door for just a few minutes. This custom became associated with Elijah, an advocate for social justice and a champion of the poor, who, legend says, visits the seder each year.

When rabbis in the Talmud could not resolve a debate about Jewish law, they would proclaim: "The Tishbi (Elijah) will solve difficult questions and problems." The tradition continues that when Elijah comes to announce the Messiah, he will answer our question and settle all disputes.[18] What question or dispute would you put before him?

WELCOMING MIRIAM

(Pour a cup of water and place it in the center of the table)

Miriam's Cup represents the living waters that sustained the Jewish people after they left Egypt. According to Midrash, as a reward for Miriam's wisdom and caring, God provided a moving well of water which followed the people throughout their wanderings in the desert. Miriam's Well was said to have healing powers that refreshed their bodies and also renewed their souls. We call on Miriam to guide us on our journey to repair the world.

Miriam the prophet,
Dance with us to repair the world.
Bring us soon your healing waters.[19]

הלל

WE SING SONGS OF PRAISE

יְיָ זְכָרָנוּ יְבָרֵךְ

יְבָרֵךְ אֶת־בֵּית יִשְׂרָאֵל יְבָרֵךְ אֶת־בֵּית אַהֲרֹן.
יְבָרֵךְ יִרְאֵי יְיָ הַקְּטַנִּים עִם הַגְּדוֹלִים.
יֹסֵף יְיָ עֲלֵיכֶם עֲלֵיכֶם וְעַל בְּנֵיכֶם.
בְּרוּכִים אַתֶּם לַייָ עֹשֵׂה שָׁמַיִם וָאָרֶץ.
הַשָּׁמַיִם שָׁמַיִם לַייָ וְהָאָרֶץ נָתַן לִבְנֵי אָדָם.
לֹא הַמֵּתִים יְהַלְלוּ־יָהּ וְלֹא כָּל־יֹרְדֵי דוּמָה.
וַאֲנַחְנוּ נְבָרֵךְ יָהּ מֵעַתָּה וְעַד עוֹלָם,
הַלְלוּיָהּ.

הַלְלוּ אֶת־יְיָ כָּל־גּוֹיִם, שַׁבְּחוּהוּ כָּל־הָאֻמִּים.
כִּי גָבַר עָלֵינוּ חַסְדּוֹ, וֶאֱמֶת יְיָ לְעוֹלָם.
הַלְלוּיָהּ.

הוֹדוּ לַייָ כִּי־טוֹב כִּי לְעוֹלָם חַסְדּוֹ.
יֹאמַר־נָא יִשְׂרָאֵל כִּי לְעוֹלָם חַסְדּוֹ.
יֹאמְרוּ נָא בֵית אַהֲרֹן כִּי לְעוֹלָם חַסְדּוֹ.
יֹאמְרוּ נָא יִרְאֵי יְיָ כִּי לְעוֹלָם חַסְדּוֹ.

אֵלִי אַתָּה וְאוֹדֶךָּ אֱלֹהַי אֲרוֹמְמֶךָּ.
הוֹדוּ לַייָ כִּי טוֹב כִּי לְעוֹלָם חַסְדּוֹ.

Praise Adonai all nations and people, for the Holy One's love for us is great and forever.

The word *halleluyah* comprises two separate words: *hallelu* which means "praise" and *Yah*, a name for God.

It says at the end of Hallel, "All Your works, Adonai our God, will praise You." This will be fulfilled when not only Israel will sing God's praises, but all beings will join in the song.[20]

HALLEL

Adonai z'charanu y'varech
Y'varech et bet Yisrael
Y'varech et bet Aharon.
Y'varech yir'ei Adonai
Hak'tanim im hag'dolim.
Yosef Adonai Aleichem
Aleichem v'al b'neichem.
B'ruchim atem l'Adonai
Oseh shamayim va'aretz.
Hashamayim shamayim l'Adonai
V'ha'aretz natan liv'nei adam.
Lo hametim y'hallelu-Ya
V'lo kol yor'dei dumah.
Va'anachnu n'varech Ya
Me'atah v'ad olam, halleluyah.

Hallelu et Adonai kol goyim
Shabchuhu kol ha'umim.
Ki gavar aleinu chasdo
V'emet Adonai l'olam halleluyah.

Hodu l'Adonai ki tov ki l'olam chasdo.
Yomar-na Yisrael ki l'olam chasdo.
Yomru-na vet Aharon ki l'olam chasdo.
Yomru-na yir'ei Adonai ki l'olam chasdo.

Eli Atah v'odeka Elohai aromemeka.
Hodu l'Adonai ki tov ki l'olam chasdo.

WE COUNT THE OMER

(Second night only)

Jewish holidays celebrate important historical moments, and many are also linked to the seasons of nature. In addition to celebrating our going out of Egypt, Passover marks the beginning of the barley harvest. On the second day of Passover, an *omer,* a sheaf of barley, was brought to the Temple as an offering. Shavuot, which comes 49 days later, commemorates the giving of the Torah, and also marks the beginning of the wheat harvest. At the second seder it is traditional to begin counting off these 49 days, referred to as the Days of the Omer.

This symbolic "countdown" from Pesach to Shavuot shows the connection between the two holidays. Our freedom from slavery was not complete until we received the Torah, which gives our lives purpose and meaning. We count the Omer with a blessing:

בָּרוּךְ אַתָּה יְיָ אֱלֹהֵינוּ מֶלֶךְ הָעוֹלָם אֲשֶׁר קִדְּשָׁנוּ בְּמִצְוֹתָיו וְצִוָּנוּ עַל סְפִירַת הָעֹמֶר.

הַיּוֹם יוֹם אֶחָד לָעֹמֶר.

Baruch Atah Adonai Eloheinu melech ha'olam, asher kid'shanu b'mitzvotav v'tzivanu al s'firat ha'omer. Hayom yom echad la'omer.

We praise You, Adonai our God, Ruler of the Universe, who makes us holy by Your mitzvot and commands us to count the Omer.

Today is the First Day of the Omer.

The goal of the Exodus was not only to make us free but also to make us a holy people. At Sinai, we agreed "to do and to listen" to the words of the Torah. Since Sinai, the Torah has been a "tree of life" that has given our people instruction and inspiration. Was there a section of Torah that you found especially meaningful this past year? Is there a section of Torah that you would like to study this coming year?

Omer "countdown" ideas for each night:

- drop a coin (except Shabbat and holidays) in a tzedakah box[21]
- count a blessing
- choose a mitzvah to do for the next day
- study a Jewish text

SEDER SONGS

אַדִּיר הוּא

אַדִּיר הוּא, אַדִּיר הוּא, יִבְנֶה בֵיתוֹ בְּקָרוֹב, בִּמְהֵרָה בִּמְהֵרָה, בְּיָמֵינוּ בְּקָרוֹב. אֵל בְּנֵה, אֵל בְּנֵה, בְּנֵה בֵיתְךָ בְּקָרוֹב.

בָּחוּר הוּא, גָּדוֹל הוּא, דָּגוּל הוּא, יִבְנֶה בֵיתוֹ בְּקָרוֹב, בִּמְהֵרָה בִּמְהֵרָה, בְּיָמֵינוּ בְּקָרוֹב. אֵל בְּנֵה, אֵל בְּנֵה, בְּנֵה בֵיתְךָ בְּקָרוֹב.

הָדוּר הוּא, וָתִיק הוּא, זַכַּאי הוּא, חָסִיד הוּא, יִבְנֶה בֵיתוֹ בְּקָרוֹב, בִּמְהֵרָה בִּמְהֵרָה, בְּיָמֵינוּ בְּקָרוֹב. אֵל בְּנֵה, אֵל בְּנֵה, בְּנֵה בֵיתְךָ בְּקָרוֹב.

טָהוֹר הוּא, יָחִיד הוּא, כַּבִּיר הוּא, לָמוּד הוּא, מֶלֶךְ הוּא, נוֹרָא הוּא, סַגִּיב הוּא, עִזּוּז הוּא, פּוֹדֶה הוּא, צַדִּיק הוּא, יִבְנֶה בֵיתוֹ בְּקָרוֹב, בִּמְהֵרָה בִּמְהֵרָה, בְּיָמֵינוּ בְּקָרוֹב. אֵל בְּנֵה, אֵל בְּנֵה, בְּנֵה בֵיתְךָ בְּקָרוֹב.

קָדוֹשׁ הוּא, רַחוּם הוּא, שַׁדַּי הוּא, תַּקִּיף הוּא, יִבְנֶה בֵיתוֹ בְּקָרוֹב, בִּמְהֵרָה בִּמְהֵרָה, בְּיָמֵינוּ בְּקָרוֹב. אֵל בְּנֵה, אֵל בְּנֵה, בְּנֵה בֵיתְךָ בְּקָרוֹב.

Mighty is God.

May Adonai's kingdom be established speedily and in our days.

God is first, great, exalted.

God is glorious, faithful, righteous, gracious.

God is pure, unique, mighty, wise, majestic, awesome, splendid, strong, redeeming, righteous.

God is holy, compassionate, almighty, and powerful.

The song Adir Hu lists attributes of God alphabetically in Hebrew. Compose a version of Adir Hu that describes God, following the English alphabet. You can start with "awesome" is God, "bold" is God, and so forth.

ADIR HU

Adir Hu, Adir Hu,
Yivneh veito b'karov
Bimherah, bimherah
B'yamenu b'karov
El b'nai El b'nai
B'nai veitcha b'karov.
Bachur Hu, Gadol Hu, Dagul Hu…
Hadur Hu, Vatik Hu, Zakkai Hu, Chassid Hu . . .
Tahor Hu, Yachid Hu, Kabir Hu, Lamud Hu . . .
Melech Hu, Norah Hu, Saggiv Hu, Izzuz Hu . . .
Podeh Hu, Tzaddik Hu . . .
Kadosh Hu, Rachum Hu, Shaddai Hu, Takif Hu . . .

אֶחָד מִי יוֹדֵעַ

אֶחָד מִי יוֹדֵעַ? אֶחָד אֲנִי יוֹדֵעַ: אֶחָד אֱלֹהֵינוּ שֶׁבַּשָּׁמַיִם וּבָאָרֶץ.

שְׁנַיִם מִי יוֹדֵעַ? שְׁנַיִם אֲנִי יוֹדֵעַ: שְׁנֵי לֻחוֹת הַבְּרִית, אֶחָד אֱלֹהֵינוּ שֶׁבַּשָּׁמַיִם וּבָאָרֶץ.

שְׁלוֹשָׁה מִי יוֹדֵעַ? שְׁלוֹשָׁה אֲנִי יוֹדֵעַ: שְׁלוֹשָׁה אָבוֹת, שְׁנֵי לֻחוֹת הַבְּרִית, אֶחָד אֱלֹהֵינוּ שֶׁבַּשָּׁמַיִם וּבָאָרֶץ.

אַרְבַּע מִי יוֹדֵעַ? אַרְבַּע אֲנִי יוֹדֵעַ: אַרְבַּע אִמָּהוֹת, שְׁלוֹשָׁה אָבוֹת, שְׁנֵי לֻחוֹת הַבְּרִית, אֶחָד אֱלֹהֵינוּ שֶׁבַּשָּׁמַיִם וּבָאָרֶץ.

חֲמִשָּׁה מִי יוֹדֵעַ? חֲמִשָּׁה אֲנִי יוֹדֵעַ: חֲמִשָּׁה חֻמְשֵׁי תוֹרָה, אַרְבַּע אִמָּהוֹת, שְׁלוֹשָׁה אָבוֹת, שְׁנֵי לֻחוֹת הַבְּרִית, אֶחָד אֱלֹהֵינוּ שֶׁבַּשָּׁמַיִם וּבָאָרֶץ.

שִׁשָּׁה מִי יוֹדֵעַ? שִׁשָּׁה אֲנִי יוֹדֵעַ: שִׁשָּׁה סִדְרֵי מִשְׁנָה, חֲמִשָּׁה חֻמְשֵׁי תוֹרָה, אַרְבַּע אִמָּהוֹת, שְׁלוֹשָׁה אָבוֹת, שְׁנֵי לֻחוֹת הַבְּרִית, אֶחָד אֱלֹהֵינוּ שֶׁבַּשָּׁמַיִם וּבָאָרֶץ.

שִׁבְעָה מִי יוֹדֵעַ? שִׁבְעָה אֲנִי יוֹדֵעַ: שִׁבְעָה יְמֵי שַׁבַּתָּא, שִׁשָּׁה סִדְרֵי מִשְׁנָה, חֲמִשָּׁה חֻמְשֵׁי תוֹרָה, אַרְבַּע אִמָּהוֹת, שְׁלוֹשָׁה אָבוֹת, שְׁנֵי לֻחוֹת הַבְּרִית, אֶחָד אֱלֹהֵינוּ שֶׁבַּשָּׁמַיִם וּבָאָרֶץ.

שְׁמוֹנָה מִי יוֹדֵעַ? שְׁמוֹנָה אֲנִי יוֹדֵעַ: שְׁמוֹנָה יְמֵי מִילָה, שִׁבְעָה יְמֵי שַׁבַּתָּא, שִׁשָּׁה סִדְרֵי מִשְׁנָה, חֲמִשָּׁה חֻמְשֵׁי תוֹרָה, אַרְבַּע אִמָּהוֹת, שְׁלוֹשָׁה אָבוֹת, שְׁנֵי לֻחוֹת הַבְּרִית, אֶחָד אֱלֹהֵינוּ שֶׁבַּשָּׁמַיִם וּבָאָרֶץ.

תִּשְׁעָה מִי יוֹדֵעַ? תִּשְׁעָה אֲנִי יוֹדֵעַ: תִּשְׁעָה יַרְחֵי לֵדָה, שְׁמוֹנָה יְמֵי מִילָה, שִׁבְעָה יְמֵי שַׁבַּתָּא, שִׁשָּׁה סִדְרֵי מִשְׁנָה, חֲמִשָּׁה חֻמְשֵׁי תוֹרָה, אַרְבַּע אִמָּהוֹת, שְׁלוֹשָׁה אָבוֹת, שְׁנֵי לֻחוֹת הַבְּרִית, אֶחָד אֱלֹהֵינוּ שֶׁבַּשָּׁמַיִם וּבָאָרֶץ.

עֲשָׂרָה מִי יוֹדֵעַ? עֲשָׂרָה אֲנִי יוֹדֵעַ: עֲשָׂרָה דִבְּרַיָּא, תִּשְׁעָה יַרְחֵי לֵדָה, שְׁמוֹנָה יְמֵי מִילָה, שִׁבְעָה יְמֵי שַׁבַּתָּא, שִׁשָּׁה סִדְרֵי מִשְׁנָה, חֲמִשָּׁה חֻמְשֵׁי תוֹרָה, אַרְבַּע אִמָּהוֹת, שְׁלוֹשָׁה אָבוֹת, שְׁנֵי לֻחוֹת הַבְּרִית, אֶחָד אֱלֹהֵינוּ שֶׁבַּשָּׁמַיִם וּבָאָרֶץ.

אַחַד עָשָׂר מִי יוֹדֵעַ? אַחַד עָשָׂר אֲנִי יוֹדֵעַ: אַחַד עָשָׂר כּוֹכְבַיָּא, עֲשָׂרָה דִבְּרַיָּא, תִּשְׁעָה יַרְחֵי לֵדָה, שְׁמוֹנָה יְמֵי מִילָה, שִׁבְעָה יְמֵי שַׁבַּתָּא, שִׁשָּׁה סִדְרֵי מִשְׁנָה, חֲמִשָּׁה חֻמְשֵׁי תוֹרָה, אַרְבַּע אִמָּהוֹת, שְׁלוֹשָׁה אָבוֹת, שְׁנֵי לֻחוֹת הַבְּרִית, אֶחָד אֱלֹהֵינוּ שֶׁבַּשָּׁמַיִם וּבָאָרֶץ.

שְׁנֵים עָשָׂר מִי יוֹדֵעַ? שְׁנֵים עָשָׂר אֲנִי יוֹדֵעַ: שְׁנֵים עָשָׂר שִׁבְטַיָּא, אַחַד עָשָׂר כּוֹכְבַיָּא, עֲשָׂרָה דִבְּרַיָּא, תִּשְׁעָה יַרְחֵי לֵדָה, שְׁמוֹנָה יְמֵי מִילָה, שִׁבְעָה יְמֵי שַׁבַּתָּא, שִׁשָּׁה סִדְרֵי מִשְׁנָה, חֲמִשָּׁה חֻמְשֵׁי תוֹרָה, אַרְבַּע אִמָּהוֹת, שְׁלוֹשָׁה אָבוֹת, שְׁנֵי לֻחוֹת הַבְּרִית, אֶחָד אֱלֹהֵינוּ שֶׁבַּשָּׁמַיִם וּבָאָרֶץ.

שְׁלוֹשָׁה עָשָׂר מִי יוֹדֵעַ? שְׁלוֹשָׁה עָשָׂר אֲנִי יוֹדֵעַ: שְׁלוֹשָׁה עָשָׂר מִדַּיָּא, שְׁנֵים עָשָׂר שִׁבְטַיָּא, אַחַד עָשָׂר כּוֹכְבַיָּא, עֲשָׂרָה דִבְּרַיָּא, תִּשְׁעָה יַרְחֵי לֵדָה, שְׁמוֹנָה יְמֵי מִילָה, שִׁבְעָה יְמֵי שַׁבַּתָּא, שִׁשָּׁה סִדְרֵי מִשְׁנָה, חֲמִשָּׁה חֻמְשֵׁי תוֹרָה, אַרְבַּע אִמָּהוֹת, שְׁלוֹשָׁה אָבוֹת, שְׁנֵי לֻחוֹת הַבְּרִית, אֶחָד אֱלֹהֵינוּ שֶׁבַּשָּׁמַיִם וּבָאָרֶץ.

ECHAD MI YODEA

Appoint a different person to sing the answer to each question. As the song builds, each person gives his/her answer in turn.

Echad mi yodea? Echad ani yodea.
Echad Eloheinu shebashamayim uva'aretz.
Shnei luchot habrit
Shloshah avot
Arba imahot
Chamishah chumshei Torah
Shishah sidrei Mishnah
Shiv'ah y'mei Shabbata…
Shmonah y'mei milah
Tishah yarchei leidah
Asarah debraya
Achad asar kochvaya
Shnem asar shivtaya
Shloshah asar midaya

Who knows ONE? I know ONE.
One is our God Who is in heaven and earth.

2: Tablets of the law
3: Fathers
4: Mothers
5: Books of Torah
6: Books of Mishnah
7: Days of the week
8: Days to circumcision
9: Months of pregnancy
10: Commandments
11: Stars in Joseph's dream
12: Tribes of Israel
13: Attributes of God

WHO KNOWS ONE ABOUT PASSOVER? [22]

1: The Passover offering brought once a year
2: Times the food is dipped
3: Matzot
4: Questions, children, cups of wine
5: Fifth cup of wine to be added when the Messiah comes
6: Items on the seder plate
7: On the 7th day the Israelites crossed the Sea of Reeds
8: Days of Passover in the diaspora
9: Things eaten or drunk at the seder
10: Plagues
11: Step 11 in the seder is… Afikomen!
12: Corridors of water the Israelites passed through at the sea
13: Verses to Echad Mi Yodea

חַד גַּדְיָא

חַד גַּדְיָא, חַד גַּדְיָא, דִּזְבַן אַבָּא בִּתְרֵי זוּזֵי, חַד גַּדְיָא, חַד גַּדְיָא.

וְאָתָא שׁוּנְרָא וְאָכַל לְגַדְיָא, דִּזְבַן אַבָּא בִּתְרֵי זוּזֵי, חַד גַּדְיָא, חַד גַּדְיָא.

וְאָתָא כַלְבָּא וְנָשַׁךְ לְשׁוּנְרָא, דְּאָכַל לְגַדְיָא, דִּזְבַן אַבָּא בִּתְרֵי זוּזֵי, חַד גַּדְיָא, חַד גַּדְיָא.

וְאָתָא חוּטְרָא וְהִכָּה לְכַלְבָּא, דְּנָשַׁךְ לְשׁוּנְרָא, דְּאָכַל לְגַדְיָא, דִּזְבַן אַבָּא בִּתְרֵי זוּזֵי, חַד גַּדְיָא, חַד גַּדְיָא.

וְאָתָא נוּרָא וְשָׂרַף לְחוּטְרָא, דְּהִכָּה לְכַלְבָּא, דְּנָשַׁךְ לְשׁוּנְרָא, דְּאָכַל לְגַדְיָא, דִּזְבַן אַבָּא בִּתְרֵי זוּזֵי, חַד גַּדְיָא, חַד גַּדְיָא.

וְאָתָא מַיָּא וְכָבָה לְנוּרָא, דְּשָׂרַף לְחוּטְרָא, דְּהִכָּה לְכַלְבָּא, דְּנָשַׁךְ לְשׁוּנְרָא, דְּאָכַל לְגַדְיָא, דִּזְבַן אַבָּא בִּתְרֵי זוּזֵי, חַד גַּדְיָא, חַד גַּדְיָא.

וְאָתָא תוֹרָא וְשָׁתָא לְמַיָּא, דְּכָבָה לְנוּרָא, דְּשָׂרַף לְחוּטְרָא, דְּהִכָּה לְכַלְבָּא, דְּנָשַׁךְ לְשׁוּנְרָא, דְּאָכַל לְגַדְיָא, דִּזְבַן אַבָּא בִּתְרֵי זוּזֵי, חַד גַּדְיָא, חַד גַּדְיָא.

וְאָתָא הַשּׁוֹחֵט וְשָׁחַט לְתוֹרָא, דְּשָׁתָה לְמַיָּא, דְּכָבָה לְנוּרָא, דְּשָׂרַף לְחוּטְרָא, דְּהִכָּה לְכַלְבָּא, דְּנָשַׁךְ לְשׁוּנְרָא, דְּאָכַל לְגַדְיָא, דִּזְבַן אַבָּא בִּתְרֵי זוּזֵי, חַד גַּדְיָא, חַד גַּדְיָא.

וְאָתָא מַלְאַךְ הַמָּוֶת, וְשָׁחַט לַשּׁוֹחֵט, דְּשָׁחַט לְתוֹרָא, דְּשָׁתָה לְמַיָּא, דְּכָבָה לְנוּרָא, דְּשָׂרַף לְחוּטְרָא, דְּהִכָּה לְכַלְבָּא, דְּנָשַׁךְ לְשׁוּנְרָא, דְּאָכַל לְגַדְיָא, דִּזְבַן אַבָּא בִּתְרֵי זוּזֵי, חַד גַּדְיָא, חַד גַּדְיָא.

וְאָתָא הַקָּדוֹשׁ בָּרוּךְ הוּא, וְשָׁחַט לְמַלְאַךְ הַמָּוֶת, דְּשָׁחַט לַשּׁוֹחֵט, דְּשָׁחַט לְתוֹרָא, דְּשָׁתָה לְמַיָּא, דְּכָבָה לְנוּרָא, דְּשָׂרַף לְחוּטְרָא, דְּהִכָּה לְכַלְבָּא, דְּנָשַׁךְ לְשׁוּנְרָא, דְּאָכַל לְגַדְיָא, דִּזְבַן אַבָּא בִּתְרֵי זוּזֵי, חַד גַּדְיָא, חַד גַּדְיָא.

CHAD GADYA

Chad gadya, chad gadya.
Dizvan aba bit'rei zuzei
Chad gadya, chad gadya.

V'ata shunra v'achal l'gadya
Dizvan aba bit'rei zuzei
Chad gadya, chad gadya.

V'ata chalba v'nashach l'shunra . . .
V'ata chutra v'hika l'chalba . . .
V'ata nura v'saraf l'chutra . . .
V'ata maya v'chava l'nura . . .
V'ata tora v'shata l'maya . . .
V'ata hashochet v'shachat l'tora . . .
V'ata Malach Hamavet v'shachat l'shochet . . .
V'ata Hakadosh Baruch Hu v'shachat
l'Malach Hamavet . . .

One little goat, one little goat
That my father bought for two zuzim.
One little goat, one little goat.
Along came a cat and ate the goat . . .
Along came a dog and bit the cat . . .
Along came a stick and beat the dog . . .
Along came a fire and burnt the stick . . .
Along came water and put out the fire . . .
Along came an ox and drank the water . . .
Along came a butcher and slaughtered the ox . . .
Along came the Angel of Death and killed the butcher . . .
Along came the Holy One and slew the Angel of Death.

Chad Gadya is an allegory describing Israel's history. The kid is Israel, purchased with two zuzim, the two tablets of the law. Next is a list of Israel's oppressors: the cat is Assyria, the dog-Babylonia, the stick-Persia, fire-Greece, water-Rome, the ox-Saracens, the butcher-the Crusaders, the Angel of Death-the Ottomans. But the song ends with an expression of hope, that the Holy One will bring peace and eternal life to the people of Israel.[23]

The chain of events may seem inexplicable, but the folk song teaches us there is a Divine order (seder) . . . even if it is a mystery to us.

נרצה WE COMPLETE THE SEDER

THE FOURTH CUP

(Lift wine cups and say)

בָּרוּךְ אַתָּה יְיָ אֱלֹהֵינוּ מֶלֶךְ הָעוֹלָם בּוֹרֵא פְּרִי הַגָּפֶן.

Baruch Atah Adonai Eloheinu melech ha'olam, borei p'ri hagafen.

We praise You, Adonai our God, Ruler of the Universe, Who creates the fruit of the vine.

(Drink the wine)

חֲסַל סִדּוּר פֶּסַח כְּהִלְכָתוֹ,
כְּכָל־מִשְׁפָּטוֹ וְחֻקָּתוֹ.
כַּאֲשֶׁר זָכִינוּ לְסַדֵּר אוֹתוֹ,
כֵּן נִזְכֶּה לַעֲשׂוֹתוֹ.
זָךְ שׁוֹכֵן מְעוֹנָה,
קוֹמֵם קְהַל עֲדַת מִי מָנָה.
בְּקָרוֹב נַהֵל נִטְעֵי כַנָּה,
פְּדוּיִים לְצִיּוֹן בְּרִנָּה.

Chasal siddur Pesach k'hilchato,
K'chol mishpato v'chukato.
Ka'asher zachinu l'sader oto
Ken nizkeh la'asoto.
Zach shochen m'onah
Komem k'hal adat mi manah.
B'karov nahel nitei chanah
P'duyim l'Zion b'rina.

Our seder is now completed.
May our service be acceptable to You, Adonai our God,
And may we be granted the blessing
Of celebrating Pesach for many years to come.
Pure and Holy One, dwelling on high,
Raise up your people with love
And lead us to Zion in joyful song.[22]

לַשָּׁנָה הַבָּאָה בִּירוּשָׁלָיִם.

Lashanah haba'ah b'Yerushalayim!

NEXT YEAR IN JERUSALEM!

Redemption requires our participation. The Midrash says that God did not split the sea until one person, Nachshon Ben Aminadav, took the first step into the water. If we take the first step, God will help us the rest of the way.

What do you think about when you say "next year in Jerusalem?"

Final *seder go-round:* What do you hope to do before next year's seder?

THE FIFTH CUP

Before concluding the seder, some families drink a fifth cup of wine in gratitude for the State of Israel.

HATIKVAH

כָּל עוֹד בַּלֵּבָב פְּנִימָה נֶפֶשׁ יְהוּדִי הוֹמִיָּה,
וּלְפַאֲתֵי מִזְרָח קָדִימָה עַיִן לְצִיּוֹן צוֹפִיָּה.
עוֹד לֹא אָבְדָה תִקְוָתֵנוּ הַתִּקְוָה בַּת שְׁנוֹת אַלְפַּיִם,
לִהְיוֹת עַם חָפְשִׁי בְּאַרְצֵנוּ אֶרֶץ צִיּוֹן וִירוּשָׁלַיִם.

Kol od balevav p'nimah,
Nefesh Yehudi homiya.
Ul'fatei mizrach kadimah
Ayin l'tzion tzofiyah.
Od lo avdah tikvatenu,
Hatikvah, bat shnot alpayim,
Li'yot am chofshi b'artzenu
Eretz Tzion v'Yerushalyim.[23]

The heart and soul of the Jew echoes the ancient hope to be a free people in the land of Zion.

FREEDOM SONGS

GO TELL IT ON THE MOUNTAIN

Go tell it on the mountain,
Over the hills and everywhere.
Go tell it on the mountain—
Let my people go!

Who are the people dressed in white?
Let my people go!
Must be the children of the Israelites--
Let my people go!

Who are the people dressed in red?
Let my people go!
Must be the people that Moses led—
Let my people go!

Add your own verses!

MOSES

There is a man come into Egypt,
And Moses is his name.
When he saw the grief upon us,
In his heart there burned a flame.
In his heart there burned a flame, O Lord,
In his heart there burned a flame.
When he saw the grief upon us,
In his heart there burned a flame.

LET MY PEOPLE GO

When Israel was in Egypt land,
Let my people go.
Oppressed so hard they could not stand,
Let my people go.
Go down, Moses, way down in Egypt land.
Tell ol' Pharaoh to let my people go.

"Thus saith the Lord," bold Moses said,
"Let my people go.
"If not I'll smite your first-born dead.
"Let my people go."
Go down, Moses, way down in Egypt land.
Tell ol' Pharaoh to let my people go.

NOTES

1 Ruth Feldstein. *Passover Seder Exchange*. Vol. 1. Passover 5747. Princeton Jewish Center.

2 Susannah Heschel suggested placing an orange on the seder plate as a symbol of inclusion. See myjewishlearning.com or ritualwell.org

3 *My Prayer* by Nissan Mindel. Merkos L'Inyonei Chinuch. Brooklyn, NW, 1978.

4 Rabbi Jeff Schein, *"Some Suggestions for a More Comfortable and Interesting Seder."*

5 Adapted from Harold Schulweis, *"No Blessing Over the Broken Matzah"* New Menorah, Spring 1990.

6 Len Douchette in Torah Aura, March 19, 21:29.

7 Adapted from *The Fifth Child* created by The National Jewish Center for Learning and Leadership.

8 This activity was suggested by Lisa and Daniel Silberman Brenner.

9 Posted by Rabbi Arthur Waskow on the Internet, August 11, 1996. Mail Havurah Digest 184.

10 Rabbi Shlomo Riskin, *The Jerusalem Post International Edition*, March 30, 1991.

11 Rabbi Yehoshua Starret. *The Breslov Haggadah*. Breslov Research Institute. Jerusaem/New York, 1989, p. 39.

12 Rabbi Marc D. Angel. *A Sephardic Passover Seder*. Hoboken: Ktav, 1988, p. 12.

13 This question was posed by Lyndall Miller at her family seder.

14 A copy of the original handwritten prayer is at the Ghetto Fighters' House in Israel.

15 Marga Hirsh suggested this custom which she and her family have followed for many years.

16 *Noah's Ark*, III:8. April 1981.

17 Deborah Ross. *Passover Instruction Kit Plan*. Jersey City: B. Manischewitz, 1963.

18 Shoshana Silberman. *Tiku Shofar.* NY: United Synagogue Commission on Jewish Education, 1993.

19 Shoshana Silberman. *The Jewish World Family Haggadah*. IBooks: 2005

20 Rabbi Nosson Scherman and Rabbi Meir Zlotowitz, eds. *The Vilna Gaon Haggadah*. Brooklyn: Mesorah Publications, 1993, pp. 78–79.

21 I learned this tzedakah idea from Rob Agus at an inter-chavurah retreat.

22 Adapted from *Olameinu, Our World*, March 1995.

23 Rabbi Morris Silverman. *Passover Haggadah*. Hartford: Prayerbook Press 1959.

24 The idea of placing Nirtzah at the very end of the seder, after the table songs, is from M. Strassfeld, *A Passover Haggadah*.

25 *Hatikvah* by Naftali Imber.

Dr. Shoshana Silberman is a consultant at the Auerbach Central Agency for Jewish Education in Philadelphia. She has been a teacher, principal, and author. Her books include *A Family Haggadah, The Whole Megillah (Almost), Tiku Shofar: A Mahzor and Sourcebook for Students and Families*, and *Siddur Shema Yisrael*. Dr. Silberman has lectured and presented workshops throughout North America on experiential Jewish education, teacher training, and staff development. She holds degrees from Columbia University, Gratz College, The University of Chicago, and Temple University. Shoshana lives in Princeton, NJ with her husband Mel. Their grown children, Shmuel, Lisa, and Gabriel, have "left the nest" but return for lively family seders and other holiday celebrations.

Katherine Janus Kahn, an illustrator, calligrapher, and sculptor, studied Fine Arts at the Bezalel School in Jerusalem and the University of Iowa. She has illustrated an impressive list of books including the acclaimed *Sammy Spider* series , a set of Family Services for Shabbat and the holidays, and many other award-winning story, activity and board books for young children. She lives in Wheaton, MD, with her husband David.

I0895159